Managing a Changing Workforce

Managing a Changing Workforce

Achieving Outstanding Service with Today's Employees

Bob Losyk

Workplace Trends Publishing Company
10396 S.W. 17th Drive
Davie, Florida 33324

1 2 3 4 5 6 7 8 9 10

ISBN 0-9647393-4-8

LCCN 95-71468

ATTENTION CORPORATIONS, UNIVERSITIES, COLLEGES, AND PROFESSIONAL ORGANIZATIONS: Quantity discounts are available on bulk purchases of this book for educational purposes or fund raising. Special books or book excerpts can also be created to fit specific needs. For information, please contact Workplace Trends Publishing Company, 10396 S.W. 17th Dr., Davie, Florida 33324 or call (305) (954 after August '96) 236-6863. Fax (305) 424-0625.

Dedication

To my wife Lois, who gave me the best love I could ever hope for; I thank you.

To my parents, Mike and Flordina, who taught me the value of education and hard work.

Acknowledgements

Many people and organizations made this book possible. First, I want to thank my wife Lois. She had faith in the project from the start and encouraged me all along the way. I am greatly indebted to her for her love and patience. In addition to her inspiration and insight, she provided many hours of researching, reading and editing, and offered countless suggestions. She took many of my thoughts and concepts and helped them come alive. It is because of her love, support, contributions, and sacrifices that this book is complete.

Next, I would like to thank my friends and colleagues who volunteered their time to read chapters and offer their helpful insights. They are all speakers, trainers, and authors who are on the cutting edge of their expertise. A special note of appreciation goes out to Bob Preziosi, a mentor to so many trainers and consultants. My thanks also go out to Lou Heckler, John Gaffin, Catherine Fyock, Jim Cathcart, Mark Sanborn, and Jerry Wilson. Their contributions were invaluable.

I would like to acknowledge my many friends and colleagues in the National Speakers Association and the American Society for Training and Development. Over the years, so many people were role models, mentors, a source of inspiration and countless ideas.

I want to acknowledge my editor, Marlene Naylor, for her excellent job. Her comments and criticisms were instrumental to the finishing touches.

I thank the many clients who have used my consulting services and the thousands of people in my audiences. The former allowed me to put concepts into action to create meaningful, positive changes in their organizations. The latter gave me a wealth of comments, examples, and feedback which helped me to crystalize my ideas and concepts which are the bedrock of this book.

Finally, there are the various CEO's and managers of the businesses mentioned in this book who are the leaders in their field. They serve as an inspiration to us all.

About the Author

Many businesses ranging from large corporations to small franchises look to Bob Losyk, M.Ed., M.B.A., when they need practical solutions for making their organizations more productive and profitable. He is a dynamic professional speaker, business consultant, and a prolific writer. As president and CEO of Innovative Training Solutions, Inc., he brings 20 years of professional insight and business savvy to his clients. Bob has been referred to as "America's Workforce Coach."

In constant demand as a speaker, trainer, and consultant, Bob addresses businesses and professional audiences worldwide on the subjects of managing and motivating the young and changing workforce, recruiting and hiring, teamwork, customer service, and sales. Subway, TCBY Yogurt, Piggly Wiggly, Marriott Corporation, American Express, I.B.M, Taco Bell, Hyatt Hotels, AAA, many national associations, and thousands of people have greatly benefited from Bob Losyk's expertise.

For information on Bob Losyk's services contact: Innovative Training Solutions, Inc., P.O. Box 290957, Ft. Lauderdale, FL 33329-0957, (305) (954 after August '96) 424-0626.

Table of Contents

Introduction

Why this Book

As we approach the turn of the century, American organizations are facing unprecedented challenges. Technology, the global economy, re-engineering, and customer demand for quality and service are all driving extraordinary changes.

At the same time, the workforce itself is going through a remarkable metamorphosis. Over the next twenty years, the workforce will be older, more female, and have the greatest number of immigrants, and people of color. The education gap will continue to grow, fueling many organizations' inabilities to find qualified, productive people. Changing values will make businesses reassess the way they hire and manage their human resources. Yet, few organizations seem ready to handle these transformations.

If you are going to be better at satisfying the most demanding of customers, you will have to be better at managing this very different workforce in a very different business climate. The old ways of hiring, and managing for service won't work. If you want to have *outstanding* service, you need to find new ways to motivate a workforce who have new beliefs, values, attitudes, and behaviors. This book is a blueprint to enable you to achieve these objectives.

How this Book Is Unique

There are a variety of good books on the demographic changes taking place in America, as well as the need for accepting and valuing diversity. Many excellent books focus on what customer service is, what customers expect, and how to give the customer what they want. My feeling is that there aren't enough books on managing your people to give *outstanding* service. Unfortunately, many service books never refer to the fact that the American workforce is no longer just White, male or female. This book looks at six major factors that are changing the profile of America's workforce. It looks at a whole new generation of workers, a generation that is here to stay; and one with very different values. It takes into account that the people you are managing to give outstanding service come from many different backgrounds and races. This book provides compelling evidence that shows you can't manage and be blind to your changing workforce.

The Origins of this Book

Many different sources inspired this book. Its content has been formulated over the last ten years. When the first books on customer service evolved in the middle 1980s, I became excited over what I saw. Suddenly, people were beginning to write about what we all experienced as shoppers and consumers. I knew there was a lot of unsatisfied customers out there that no one was paying much attention to. I also realized that many businesses needed help in making positive changes to solving customer problems.

I saw an opportunity and started my consulting practice. My early years were spent strictly in training and consulting in the area of customer service in South Florida. As I spent many hours and days in South Florida's corporations, I realized that the workforce here was a melting pot of many different values, cultures, and ethnic backgrounds. I saw how this affected people's abilities to work together, as well as to serve the customer, both positively and negatively. I saw how diversity positively impacted the brainstorming and problem solving sessions we accomplished in my seminars.

As my business evolved from a local to an international business, and I became in demand as a speaker at conventions, I began hearing from my audiences that their work force was also changing, both in demographics and in values.

I began researching the workforce and the many changes that were taking place. The book, *Workforce 2000: Work and Workers for the 21st Century* (Johnston and Packer, 1987), gave me the realization that the changes ahead were to be dramatic and permanent. I realized that if we were to have good customer service, we would have to take into account those changes. Managers and owners could not continue doing things the same way they did in the sixties and seventies. Those management practices were no longer in step with the workforce. If we were really to solve customer problems, then we had to find some new methods.

For the past eight years I developed my ideas and presented them in hundreds of keynote speeches and seminars, which were given to large corporations, professional associations, small businesses, franchises, and educational institutions. The attendees ranged from front line, supervisors, and managers of all levels, to presidents and CEO's.

Many of the ideas in this book came from the participants themselves. In the research I conduct before each program, they shared their experiences, stories, and expertise with me. In my seminars, their creative ideas surfaced during the brainstorming and problem solving sessions.

This book blends together the theory with real and specific examples compiled over the years. The attempt has been made to keep the suggestions as practical as possible, so that you can read, and readily implement them. The book is for organizations and institutions of all sizes, both public and private, and should be read by presidents, CEO's, small business and franchise owners, and managers and supervisors of all levels.

How the Book Is Arranged

The chapters are placed in a logical, progressive order and are designed to build upon each other. Each chapter, beginning with chapter two, has tips at the end for a review or quick reference.

Chapter one describes the six major changes affecting today's diverse workplace. Each description of change is followed by the effects and implications caused by those changes. It then suggests a list of action ideas to implement.

Chapter two deals with how management's role has changed over the years from one of being an autocratic organizer and controller, to one of being more of a leader, supporter, provider, facilitator and coach.

Chapter three looks at the next generation, known as "Generation X'ers," "baby busters," or "Yiffies." It describes their values, and how they are different from previous generations. This chapter offers suggestions to motivate the next generation that have been proven over many years. It utilizes many of the ideas used by my clients who hire young workers almost exclusively and have had great success. This group is taken as a whole, being segmented only by age. Other chapters discuss the diversity of the workforce and how to manage for these employees.

Chapter four discusses new ways to recruit employees and unusual places to look for them. It goes into detail on the hiring process. It takes you through an interview, step by step. Managing people for outstanding service starts with hiring the right people.

Chapter five shows you how to create service standards. If you don't establish, monitor, and measure customer related standards of behavior you will never give outstanding customer service. Instead, you will only give lip service.

Chapter six takes you through the basic considerations prior to training your staff to give outstanding service. It will tell you who to train, and what subjects to train employees in, when and where to train, how to train, and why that training must be continually reinforced. People will do things the way you want them to only if they are trained properly.

Chapter seven is all about that buzzword "empowerment." However, it's not just a buzzword. It is a very critical step after training. Empowerment is giving your people the awesome responsibility to take action on your behalf to satisfy the customer.

Chapter eight discusses teamwork. With the workforce being so diverse, it is difficult to get different people to work together. This chapter deals with the characteristics of effective teams, and the steps managers must take to create teams that will enhance service.

Chapter nine is about a crucial element in managing for outstanding service: high quality feedback. When properly given, it creates a learning and motivating experience. When improperly given, it creates resentment, poor service, and turnover. The chapter explains how to give feedback that corrects behavior and how to verbally reinforce exceptional behavior.

The final chapter provides you with a system for rewarding and recognizing your employees for outstanding service. It takes you step-by-step through designing a program. It explains the guidelines and conditions that make it effective and gives many specific examples of rewards and recognition that work.

A Footnote

In various chapters, I have given you information on handling certain situations with people from diverse backgrounds, or about immigrants who have recently arrived. Many ideas have come from managers I have interviewed who found these methods effective. I don't pretend to have all the answers to deal with all of the problems.

It is impossible to mention every race or diverse group that have come to our shores. Therefore, I took the liberty of mentioning African Americans, Asian Americans and Hispanic Americans. The lack of space prevents me from listing all possible groups.

When discussing immigrant work groups, I discuss communication and language barriers. I do not wish to imply that all immigrants who enter our great country have no knowledge of the language. Some can't speak any English, but many are fluent in English and we have all experienced the varying degrees between the two extremes.

I regret, however, any misunderstandings or misstatements in this area.

When managing people from diverse backgrounds, it is important to remember that not every technique works the same way for every group or individual. Although a specific group, sex, or generation may have common characteristics or motivations, these are only trends or generalizations. Your challenge is to be fair and consistent with that group, but at the same time manage them as individuals. Each person has his or her own unique needs, and each must be managed accordingly.

By the end of this book, you will have an effective design for managing a changing workforce to give *outstanding* service. But, just as the workforce is changing, we have to change our ways of managing. Your success with your customers is contingent upon what you do after you read the book.

How the Workforce Is Changing

"I have to be really creative in my recruiting because there is such a lack of qualified entry level service people out there," says Marsha, a human resource manager for a chain of auto parts stores.

"We only hire senior citizens now. We find they're more productive and dependable," states Todd, a reservations manager for a hotel chain.

"We have hired many women over the past five years and with great results. But they advance very slowly into key management positions so a lot of them leave. It creates a turnover problem, and it really hurts service," laments Anne, a director of operations for a retail outlet chain.

"No one will take the jobs we have to offer. It's beneath them to do physical labor. They would rather be on welfare and work odd jobs on the side. So we recruit newly arrived immigrants with green cards. They're hard workers. Of course, this creates a language and communication problem," comments Dave, owner of a wood pallet manufacturing firm.

"The people coming out of school are computer whizzes, but they just don't have the analytical skills that we need in today's high tech environment, and they don't have the interpersonal skills we need for communicating with our

customers," concludes Mai-Ling, a department head for a Silicon Valley high-tech firm.

"Today's young people drive us crazy! It's almost as if they came from outer space. They have absolutely no idea what work ethic is all about and want to have fun all the time. Customer service is a foreign language to them," exclaims Fernando, owner of six fast food restaurants.

These are actual quotes from people in businesses all across the country. What is going on here? Is the workforce so different than ten or twenty years ago? Why can't we find good people, keep them, and motivate them to give outstanding service? Is this a discouraging preview of what the future holds?

The answers to these questions lie in understanding the changes going on today; changes that will continue well into the future. You can't understand the future unless you accurately perceive the present. If you look at the present workforce, you can see that the trends of the future workforce are here today. It is already a reality in organizations throughout America. You can expect these trends to grow for the next two decades, impacting American organizations in an unprecedented way. Those organizations that understand how today's workforce is changing will be able to adapt. They will be the leaders in attracting, hiring, and maintaining good service people.

Forces Shaping the Future

Six critical forces are reshaping and redefining the American workforce and workplace today. Johnston and Packer, acting as project directors for the landmark study from the Hudson Institute, entitled *Workforce 2000: Work and Workers for the 21st Century* have documented four of these demographic forces. They include:

1. The population and workforce is in a very slow growth period.

2. The average age of the American worker is older than almost any time in history, and at the same time there are less young workers entering the workforce.

3. More and more women will be entering the workforce than ever before.

4. Ethnic diversity is growing at an unprecedented rate (Johnston & Packer, 1987, pp. 75-76).

5. At the same time, the education gap continues to expand between the current workforce, and the workforce needed in the future (National Center on Education and the Economy, 1990).

6. The values that people once had are changing. The workforce is comprised of people with a real mix of values, working side by side (Jamieson & O'Mara, 1991). These values are often being reshaped by forces outside the worker's control.

Couple these six forces with the changing nature of work being shaped by technological advances; the realities of competing in a global economy, along with customers' demands for quality and service; and you have a very different workforce competing in a very different workplace.

These changes have confused, upset, and even angered managers and business owners. In my discussions with management around the country, I have noticed a fear and anxiety about the changes. This is often due to a sinking feeling of not being in control of their own destiny.

Each of these forces and their effects on the workplace will be examined in this chapter. When viewed together, they provide a picture of a workforce and workplace in the next ten to twenty years that will be unlike any ever seen before. At the end of each section, I will give you some brief tips that can help in dealing with the changes that lie ahead.

Slow Growth of the Population and Workforce

The U.S. population will grow about three-fourths of one percent a year during the next twenty years. This rate is far slower than at any time in our history, other than the depression era. This slow growth of population will be mirrored by the slowest growth in our labor force since the 1930s, a rate of only one percent (Johnston & Packer, p. 75-78).

Effect on the Workplace

As a result, the labor market will tighten up. This will cause economic growth to fall below the three percent rate of the 1960s and 1970s. In my phone surveys, many managers and owners complain that they can't find enough good entry-level people who are willing to work for the wages they are offering. Faced with increasing entry level shortages, or a need for special skills, employers are often forced to demand higher productivity from employees. Many of today's workers already complain they are being forced to do more in less time than ever before. They often are stressed out by the end of each workday.

Because of demand, more employers are beginning to hire underutilized workers. This group includes (but is not limited to) minorities, disabled workers, displaced workers (from mergers, downsizing, closings), those with limited skills, temporary or part-time employees, retirees, and re-entries, such as mothers whose children are older and in school. Organizations that never looked at these employees before will be forced to do so. They will have to hire a certain number of people to get the job done. That number will include people in all of these groups.

Ideas to Implement

- Frequently assess the changing composition of your workforce.
- Prepare for less qualified entry-level workers through effective on-the-job training.

- Create plans to extend the retirement age and keep older workers.

- Create a strategic plan to find, hire, and train under utilized and non-traditional workers.

- Improve hiring practices through better interview methods and employee assessments.

- Adjust management practices and procedures to accommodate the bulge of older workers.

- Train supervisors and managers to be better leaders and motivators, in order to decrease turnover.

America Is Aging

Between 1946 and 1964, 76 million Americans were born. As this baby boom generation now enters middle age, the average age of employees will reach 41 years by 2020 (Pilenzo, 1990). This age will be higher than any other period in our nation's history.

Between 1986 and the year 2000, the number of people between 48 and 53 years of age will jump by an astonishing 67%! At the same time, the number of people under 30 years of age will shrink. Their share of the population will decrease from 18% to 13%. (Johnston & Packer, pp. 79-80).

The "baby buster" generation, those following the "baby boomers," are much smaller as a group than their "boomer" predecessors. This group, born between 1965 and 1976, numbers 41 million, not including the 3 million who have immigrated from other countries (Dunn, 1993).

Effect on the Workplace

Many older workers will find that economic necessity will force them to work far beyond the normal retirement age. With advances in healthcare and medical technology, many older workers will be able to contribute as never before. The middle aged and older workers will be the heart of our American workforce.

Berkshire Hathaway's Chairman, Warren Buffet, was prodded about the age of one his company presidents. Rose

Blumkin had just turned 94. He stated, "She is clearly gathering speed and may well reach her full potential in another five or ten years. Therefore, I've persuaded the board to scrap our mandatory retirement at age 100 policy." Buffett's comments point out how many seniors feel about their abilities and that of their peer group (Training & Development Journal, Feb., 1990, p. 24).

Author Ken Dychtwald, Founder and Chairman of Age Wave, Inc. states some people may never retire, or they may retire many times. People will stop working to pursue other interests and then come back into the workforce. The shortage of qualified young people will make this possible.

Dychtwald also states that because of the growing number of older workers, and the power they will have, the workplace will be dramatically altered. Benefits such as "sabbaticals, phased retirement programs, flex time, job banks, and career-transition retraining programs will be geared to older workers" (Training & Development Journal, Feb., 1990, p. 24).

The United States will have a segment of an older population who are educated, stable, and highly productive. However, organizations will have to pay more in salaries and benefits to attract this group. Some older workers may be squeezed out of their jobs as companies scramble to remain competitive. As the baby boomers begin retiring around 2005, they will also begin to take their benefits and pensions with them. This will also add to the challenge of businesses staying profitable.

Many organizations who almost exclusively hire the young workforce (retailers, restaurants), and experience high turnover may begin to rethink their policies. There may not be enough *qualified* young ones to go around.

Those organizations that have hired retirees and senior citizens have found it to be very profitable. Companies such as the Days Inn of America began hiring senior citizens as their reservationists in order to cut down on turnover. Not only was turnover lowered, but lateness and absenteeism were dramatically reduced. Days Inn also found that it cost less to train the older workers than the young ones. One study by the Commonwealth Fund in 1991 found that older workers stay on the job longer and also give better customer service. They were also rated higher by management in such key areas as productivity, loyalty, reliability, and stability.

The very young and relatively old will be working side by side as a result of the dwindling workforce. In some cases, the very young will be, and presently are, managing the old. The reverse situation will still continue but to a lesser degree. Great differences between these two groups in education, values, and experiences will breed definite and predictable communication gaps. Training in working with older employees will become imperative for the young, as well as training for the older employees in communicating with the young.

I was retained by a telemarketing company that set a goal for 100% customer satisfaction. Their telephone sales staff consisted totally of employees 18-25 years of age, except for two older men in their sixties who recently lost jobs with other companies due to re-engineering. I asked the young workers what it was like to work with the two men. They stated, "Terrible, they think they know it all, and you can't tell them a thing."

I asked the two older men what it was like to work with the younger people. They said, "Terrible, they think they know it all, and you can't tell them a thing." When we sat down and discussed the issues that separated them, we found it was due to the differences in values between the "baby buster" and "radio generation." The stereotypes about each other's value system were creating a barrier that prevented them from working together. When we brought this out and implemented a system for conflict management, the problem was eliminated. With the young and old working side by side, it becomes increasingly important to address the issue of inter-generational conflict and to provide training to deal with it.

Ideas to Implement

- Create a recruitment policy for older and retired workers.
- Train and retrain older workers for today's jobs.
- Train managers to lead and coach older workers.
- Train other generations about working with senior employees.
- Be sensitive to the needs of older workers and create benefits specific to their age group.
- Change the nature of the job to prevent boredom and burnout.
- Be flexible in scheduling as older workers have other interests outside of the workplace.
- Provide support and assistance to ensure success.
- Have older workers track their own productivity and progress.
- Create a reward system specific to the needs and values of older workers.
- Create and implement a strategic plan for recruiting and hiring young, qualified people.
- Create compensation and benefit plans designed specifically for people at different stages in their life.

Increase in Female Workers

According to figures from a study in November 1993 from the U.S. Bureau of Labor Statistics, females are projected to make up 63.2% of the workforce by the year 2005. Over three-fifths of all women will be employed. However, this growth of females may taper off after the year 2005 and will contribute to the shortage of available workers in the next century.

Effect on the Workplace

Many of America's workplace policies were created during a time when men were the breadwinners and decision makers, and women stayed home to raise a family. Organizations need to reform these policies to fit today's workforce. If companies are going to overcome future labor shortages, many women's issues relating to the family must be addressed now. These include: maternity leave, day care, healthcare benefits, part-time and flex-time options, job-sharing, child emergency care, elder care, and dual career couples. Benefits must be restructured to accommodate both the single and double wage earning families.

Companies such as Barnett Bank, Inc. of Jacksonville, are leading the way in support of a work and family balance for women. In a statewide search done by the Florida Commission on the Status of Women, Barnett Bank was recently voted the most woman-friendly company in the state of Florida. Just a few of the ways Barnett accomplishes this is by transporting children of workers after school to their day care centers, tracking women into high positions, and having a health maintenance organization at their headquarters. With 30,000 employees, Barnett spends a minimum of $70.00 per year for each employee to help achieve that balance (Barciela, June 14, 1995).

Today, women are looking for flexibility in the workplace to enable them to take care of their families. If they are going to be committed to an employer, they must have a boss and a company that is family supportive. Women need to be able to handle medical emergencies, doctor and dentist appointments and go to school programs and meetings for their children. When they are thinking about the needs of their children, they won't be thinking about customers' needs.

It is difficult for women to juggle two jobs: the home and the office. Many are choosing to cut back hours or leave completely. The number of part time female workers, as well as those working at home, will increase as women attempt to better integrate their jobs with raising children. More women with children now seek to work less hours.

A recent Gallup poll indicated that only 13% of working women with children want to work a full time job. Sixty percent want to work only part-time, and 16% do not want to work at all.

A recent USA Today, survey showed that 96% of 1,278 respondents would actually take a pay cut in order to spend more time with their families (Peterson, 1995). The message is clear. People are undergoing a change in attitudes about families. They are expressing both a desire and commitment to parenting and the family. Woman want to spend more time raising their children because they have seen the results of years of latchkey children and its negative effects.

As the proportion of female workers grows, so does the proportion of women who leave due to the "glass ceiling" or barrier that prevents them from advancing into executive levels. Organizations of all sizes have failed to halt this exodus. They spend so much money on hiring and training females, yet put into place promotion and advancement policies that drive them out the door!

Ironically, there is evidence that women make better managers than their male counterparts. Their leadership styles are different than that of men. Men tend to be more authoritarian, whereas women tend to be more open, and they invite involvement and participation. "They are likely to be seen as more effective and satisfying as leaders by both their male and female followers. Unfortunately, the glass ceiling may keep organizations from the best use of their management potential, and perhaps it is time the glass ceiling was shattered" (Bass & Avolio, 1994).

The gaps between male and female wages for equal work, plus inequities in promotion policies must be rectified. One survey of over 400 female managers (Business Week, June 8, 1992) found that over half of the managers thought that the progress previously made with regard to hiring and promotion of women was slowing. Over 70% saw the male-dominated top management of corporations as being a major obstacle to success. The number of women in top positions has not risen in proportion to the number of females workers. Companies must identify those women with high potential early on and create a system for mentoring and advancing them.

Many women leave to start their own small businesses, often out of the home. According to a recent Dun & Bradstreet Information Services survey, female owned American businesses now employ more people than do the Fortune 500 companies around the world.

One study of five hundred female entrepreneurs found their ages averaged between thirty-five and forty-five years. These women who were in their prime years to work their way up the corporate ladder chose to go out on their own (Therrien, Carson, Hamilton, & Hurlock, 1986). These entrepreneurs found they can balance work and family needs better.

Savvy companies that lead in these areas can use their reputation as a workplace that is dedicated to family support in order to gain good employees. Those that have a reputation for not caring about their people and their families will be unable to recruit candidates who find this to be a top priority.

Employers must pay attention to the needs of their female employees and view women as an asset, and not a cost. They need to create policies and practices that give women more options and choices to balance their lives. They need to show female employees that they are valued and so are their families.

Ideas to Implement

- Create a policy for recruiting, hiring, and retaining female employees.
- Eliminate the gap between men and women's salaries and benefits.
- Eliminate sexist terms, policies, and behaviors.
- Create a task force to find out what women want and need.
- Rethink and revamp leave policies for pregnancy, childbirth, and the first three years.

- Rethink transfer policies for dual-career families.
- Rethink family-sensitive policies concerning, childcare, child and school emergencies, and elder care.
- Create alternate and flexible work schedules with part-time workers, job sharing, flexi-scheduling, and working at home.
- Examine your benefits policy for single mothers.
- Create a support group for single mothers.
- Create the same opportunities for women as men in moving up the corporate ladder (e.g. mentoring).
- Create a mentoring program for women.
- Put more women on corporate boards to display commitment.
- Encourage and reward female involvement in women's professional groups in the community.
- Institute a sexual harassment policy.

Ethnic Diversity

Prior to the 1970s, the major growth in population was among white men and women. The work force was dominated by the White American male. For at least the next twenty years, 85% of the U.S. population growth will be comprised of non-white groups such as African Americans, Asian Americans, and Hispanic Americans (U.S. Bureau of Census, 1990).

Unless the current cry for immigration reform takes place, between 600,000 and one million legal and illegal immigrants will enter the workforce annually. The U.S. will continue to be a powerful magnet for those who seek refuge or opportunity.

Asian and Hispanic populations will double over the next twenty years, with many immigrants moving to the same geographic locations as their predecessors. Non-whites, women, and immigrants will comprise five-sixths of the net addition to the workforce (Johnston & Packer).

By 2010, at the latest, (some estimates are sooner), the White American male will be the new minority.

Effect on the Workplace

Management must learn to value the differences and the creativity and richness that diversity brings to the workplace. They need to get the most from people who are different. Unfortunately many of today's management trends were created for an all white, male workforce. Lennie Copeland, a producer of diversity training videos states, "With a multicultural workforce, management fads . . . are a real problem. They are based on assumptions of a white male workforce, white male motivations, white male behavior, and white male values" (Copeland, 1989 pp. 17-18). As the workforce changes, so must those management trends.

A multicultural and bilingual workforce makes good business sense. Organizations need to hire a diverse spectrum of people to solve problems with a customer base that is increasingly multicultural and more global. Management can't properly respond to customers from different ethnic backgrounds if they have an all white, English-speaking workforce. Diversity must be recognized from a different point of view and seen as a unique competitive edge. This edge is an advantage in today's global marketplace.

Many different ethnic groups working together create a broad spectrum of issues and challenges for today's managers. Companies must identify the assumptions and misconceptions they have in their testing, hiring, orientation, training, and rewarding of different ethnic groups. These misconceptions often prevent them from hiring diverse people or decrease their ability to manage different groups effectively.

Organizations that have hired mostly White American males and have resisted change, will have to look elsewhere. Well educated and highly trained minorities will be in great demand. Organizations must seize the initiative and become proactive in recruiting diverse candidates.

Organizations that have traditionally overlooked African Americans, Asian Americans, Hispanic Americans, and others, for whatever reasons, will need to reach out to them as never before. Policies and practices need to be examined and rethought about how African Americans and these other groups are hired and promoted. The same opportunities that exist for whites must be made available to all people of all races, both male and female. The same glass ceiling that prevents African Americans and other people of color from moving up the corporate ladder has to be eliminated. To achieve this, mentoring programs must be instituted, with white males and females mentoring African American, and other groups.

Despite the cultural differences, many immigrant groups have come here to better themselves economically. They are very motivated and work hard at their jobs. In company after company that we have interviewed, the blue collar immigrant worker is a valuable asset to their workforce and often take the jobs American workers don't want.

In many cases they are the only people willing to do the physical labor of working in the fields. They are the ones who pick the fruits and vegetables we eat, put the roofs on our houses, and build the roads. They help keep prices down and don't take jobs away from others (Garvin, 1995).

The scientists, engineers, and other highly educated immigrants who arrive often fill jobs where there is a shortage of qualified workers. One writer estimates that at every major high-tech company in the U.S., over half the "crucial players" are foreign-born. These, in particular, are the people who actually design and create the hardware and software products (Garvin, 1995).

Another sizable challenge that diversity brings is the need for cross-cultural awareness. The more diversity increases, the more cultural and communications gaps will develop. If diverse people are placed in entry level positions, it will be critical for them to work together effectively to serve customers. Disrespect, lack of trust, stress, and infighting will only bring down the level of service, quality, and productivity. People must be trained to understand each other, and deal with each other's differences.

Managers will need to be trained in how to lead and motivate diverse people.

A small, but important example: non-Hispanics need to understand that Hispanics do not like to be lumped together because they have a common language. They are separated by different origins, dialects, cultures, values, cuisine, and the number of years spent in the United States. One Hispanic group may know very little about another Hispanic group. In fact, some get insulted when they are compared to each other. For example, Cuban Americans, although respectful of other groups, consider themselves very different from Puerto Rican Americans or Mexican Americans, and do not wish to be lumped together with other Hispanic groups.

Asian Americans are also often lumped together as one group. Again, they are very different, with each group having its own distinct country, culture, and heritage. Many Asian groups understand very little about other Asian groups. They can't communicate due to language differences. It is very important for managers and co-workers not to stereotype them as one group but to treat them as individuals.

Another issue is that many immigrants lack knowledge of the American workplace. This quickly becomes apparent. This can be solved by offering training that enables these groups to become acculturated in understanding the attitudes and behaviors expected on the job.

Ideas to Implement

- Respect and value the differences that diversity brings.
- Commit to the elimination of prejudice and discrimination.
- Create a policy to recruit and hire people from diverse cultures.
- Recognize that language barriers may be formidable and set up English language training.
- Provide acculturation for those unfamiliar with American workplace values or American lifestyles.

- Provide remedial education for those who were previously deprived.

- Provide cross-cultural training to foster understanding.

- Train managers in leading and motivating different ethnic groups

- Train employees and managers in conflict resolution.

- Create culture-specific rewards as motivators.

- Reduce cultural biases in performance standards that prevent African Americans, Hispanics, Asian Americans, and others from receiving promotions. Be sensitive to helpful policies toward immigrant groups that isolate or ignore African Americans or Native Americans.

- Create incentives and rewards for bringing in high quality friends and relatives.

The Growing Education Gap

One recent study by the University of Pennsylvania for the Department of Education indicates that a third of the businesses surveyed said 25% or more of their workers "were not fully proficient in their jobs." At the same time, 57% of the employers said the quality of skills they required had increased in the last three years. The employers have extreme doubts that the high schools and colleges can adequately prepare people for today's jobs (New York Times Service, 1995).

Following the turn of this century, more than half of all jobs will need more than a high school education. Almost one third will require a college degree. Technical, managerial, sales, and service jobs will grow faster than all other job categories. Many jobs may go unfilled as a result of the lack of qualified people. At the same time, many jobs such as blue collar supervisors, assemblers, hand workers, and machine operators will drop dramatically (Johnston & Packer, p.97).

The greatest growth of future jobs will be in the service sector. Many of these jobs will require technical, analytical, and interpersonal skills. At the same time, entry level younger workers in the next twenty years will come from a myriad of ethnic backgrounds. The challenge is how do you educate and train these individuals and match them to the job requirements? This challenge is a formidable one.

Effect on the Workplace

The mix of skills needed in the next twenty years will rise higher than ever before. The gap between the skills that we have and the skills we need in the workplace will expand greatly. New jobs being created demand a solid background in mathematics, statistics, logic, creativity, and analytical skills.

"In Workplace 2000, the most valuable commodity will be knowledge and the pulsating flow of ideas exchanging, interacting, and expanding. To participate in the game, Americans will have to possess the requisite skills" (Boyett & Conn, 1991, p. 278). It won't be enough for employees to absorb information. They must be able to analyze it, interpret it, and then make decisions.

This shift in skills is being created by the decline of the country as a manufacturing society, towards one that is driven by the processing of information in a service-based society. The new rules demand quality, service, and support to the customer when they want it. America can't meet the standards and demands of its customers without a skilled and trained workforce. According to Anthony Carnevale, chairperson of the National Commission on Employment Policy, "If America doesn't supply these things to its customers, somebody else will" (Carnevale, 1990, p. 4).

In the service fields, employees will need to have a good basic education. They will need to know how to read and interpret information, understand the basics of mathematics, and know how to communicate. The emphasis will be on both computer and interpersonal skills. Young workers lacking those skills will find it increasingly harder to obtain entry level service jobs. The educationally disadvantaged immigrant as well as the high school drop out, or those that barely got by will have a rough road ahead, competing for the same scarce jobs. For the un-skilled worker, the opportunities look bleak. The millions of functionally illiterate will have a hard time finding adequate employment.

This will create a difficult paradox. Many employers will be looking for qualified, educated people and will have trouble finding them. Large numbers of unqualified people will be looking for jobs, yet few employers will want to chance hiring them.

The gap will grow between the haves and have-nots. It is difficult enough for college graduates to find jobs paying the wages desired. To not graduate high school is almost inviting financial disaster for many. For a young man today to make what a young man made in the 1970s, a college degree or technical school degree is required. Women have fared better, partly because they are working more hours (Zalvidar, 1995).

David Kearns, former C.E.O. of Xerox Corporation was very candid about the lack of qualified and trained workers in America. He stated, "American businesses will have to hire a million new workers a year who can't read, write, or count. Teaching them how, and absorbing the lost produc-tivity while they are learning will cost industry $25 billion a year for as long as it takes" (Miller, 1988, pp. 47-52).

To say that a large number of unemployable people can't be used in so many unfilled jobs is more than a tragedy. It is a national disaster. But, in reality, there are only two choices: train the people yourself or go without the workers. Since going without means not going at all, many companies may be forced to hire totally unqualified, illiterate workers. The costs to educate them could be staggering. Employers will have to invest heavily to create the workforce they want and need.

Ideas to Implement

- Approach employee training and education as an ongoing process.
- Assess how much training is now being done, or what is spent on training per person.

- Begin preparing now for the training and retraining that is critical to your organization's future.
- Identify critical and immediate areas for training, particularly in customer service.
- Create a training budget based on needs assessment.
- Increase training in remedial and basic education.
- Set up an educational library with computer-based modules, books, video and audiotapes.
- Measure the effects after the training.
- Work with local school districts for effective change that links the world of school and work together.
- Reward people for learning new job skills.
- Treat training as an investment with a very high return.
- As a manager or owner, be the vocal champion of training and its benefits.

Changing Values

Today's workers have a wide mix of values. "It is perhaps important to understand that values have proliferated; older ones have not necessarily been replaced by others. More values are represented and they are more widely dispersed" (Jamieson & O'Mara, p. 29).

In many cases, we can see a division of values along generational lines. But these are trends, and there are always exceptions. Many people have priorities very different than those of the past. People have become more inner-directed and are looking for more self-fulfillment. Many people no longer live to work but work to live. They no longer make work the entire center of their lives. Work is just a means to getting other things you need. For many individuals, personal development, leisure time, and quality family time have become more important than company goals or loyalty.

Challenging work, job satisfaction, a sense of achievement, respect, and recognition for a job well done have become the main elements people desire from their jobs. In addition, people want some sense of control. They want to be in charge of their own destinies, both inside and outside of the workplace.

Mergers, downsizing, and re-engineering have reaped havoc and fear on today's workers. People wonder why they should be loyal to companies that are laying them off in droves. Young workers have seen their parents give thirty or more years of loyalty to one company only to have a security guard help them clean out their desks and walk them out the door. Cynicism has become rampant.

Workers often feel alienated from management and owners that don't understand their wants and needs, don't care about their employees inside or outside of work, and often don't even like them if they are different in any way. Yet, management expects employees to care about their business and their customers.

Another issue in the workplace is the effect of different generations working side by side. With three different generations of employees working together, there can often be a predictable clash of values. Different generations have different experiences and education levels. They have different values with which they were raised. When there are young workers ("Generation X'ers") working along side the "baby boomers," or the older "radio generation," there is bound to be some conflict.

Although there are many exceptions to the rule, there are some trends in the values of these three generations. The radio generation, sometimes known as the "World War II generation" or "traditionalists" were born between 1925 and 1945. They are a very conservative age group, with a heavy accent on following the rules and the chain of command. They are used to doing things the same old way. The main events that shaped their life were the Great Depression and World II. Their heroes were Presidents Harry Truman and Dwight D. Eisenhower, and any number of other World War II generals. Their motivators in the work place are security and a comfortable retirement. Their value system is in greatest conflict with the workplace of the 90s and will be increasingly so into the next decade.

The "baby boomers" were born between 1946 to 1964. They are much more liberal as a group and at the same time altruistic and moralistic. They broke away from many of the traditions of their parents, as can be seen by the idealistic hippie movement of the sixties. They are a generation that immersed themselves in their careers. Materials possessions and money are their prime motivators. Rock and roll music, TV, and the Vietnam War shaped their lives. Their heroes were the Kennedys and Martin Luther King. The boomers have felt the greatest effects from the corporate downsizing and layoffs of the early '90s. As a result, many have redirected their priorities towards the family instead of the workplace.

"Generation X'ers" or the "baby busters" are rather paradoxical. Born after 1964, they have broken away from many of the ideals their parents hold dear, but yet retain some of the others and don't like to admit it. They are self-absorbed, cynical, and highly competitive. They are very much at home with computers and high-tech gadgets. The historical events that shaped their lives were Watergate and the Persian Gulf War. Their heroes are often rock and movie stars. Their prime motivators in the workplace are rewards, recognition, and challenges. They don't want to wait long to get what they want. They have less loyalty to an employer than the previous generations. They will be discussed in greater detail in Chapter Three.

Effect on the Workplace

If you are to survive in managing today's workforce and have them care about your customers, then you must recognize the new reality. The radio generation, who often gave unquestioning loyalty, is retiring. With them will go their value system. In the past, managers could demand loyalty and commitment from them. Part of the reason was because management controlled events totally. Today, too many other factors such as corporate boards, technology, and global realities now control events.

With mergers, acquisitions, re-engineering and downsizing, the "baby busters" have found it doesn't pay to be loyal as the two generations preceding them. "The generations before them, steeped in the tradition of the American work ethic, prided themselves on their loyalty and commitment to the organization. Both groups looked at their jobs and careers as a kind of religious metaphor, in which hard work was the way to salvation—in this case, job security, material goods, and a pension" (Doyle, 1993, p. 76).

The "Generation X'ers" are less committed. For them, the loyalty and commitment is not there from management. Management must find a way to get it back in spite of the need to restructure. It is this very loyalty and commitment that made companies successful in the past.

Loyalty and commitment are a response to listening to your people and valuing their opinions. But, loyalty and commitment are two-way streets. If you want to have it, you have to give it. One way to quell employee fears and build loyalty and commitment is through listening, employee involvement, and taking care of your people.

The corporate restructuring and trend towards cross-functional teams have created situations where three generations of workers may be working side by side. This age diversity, although it brings a fresh approach to solving problems, also creates conflict. "All this mixing and matching often brings a wider breadth of experience and ideas to the business at hand. But it can also create a clash of cultures the likes of which management have rarely dealt with before" (Murphy, 1991, p. 44).

Top management has largely ignored this clash. In order to bring about mutual understanding between the generations, management has to learn to be flexible. Managers must learn what kind of structure and work environment each generation thrives in and then create that atmosphere for them. There is also a need to create mentoring programs where different age groups can mentor each other. This eliminates biases and creates understanding and closer working relationships.

Finally, management must open up the lines of communication in all directions. As George Bernard Shaw once said, "The trouble with communication is the illusion that it has been accomplished." People have the need to know what is going on, and how they fit into the big picture. Open communication lets people know how they are doing as individuals and teams. It also fosters comraderie and helps in eliminating age biases. Never assume your people have heard the messages you are trying to get across. Keep the communication channels open back to you, so you are sure your people get those messages.

Ideas to Implement

- Look at employees as an asset, rather than a cost.
- Find out what motivates each person individually and link these motivations with workplace rewards.
- Listen and value peoples opinions.
- Keep people totally informed; share information.
- Get people involved in decision-making.
- Create an employee suggestion system.
- Give people more options and choices in their everyday work.
- Use attitude surveys to better understand your people.
- Eliminate inter-generational value conflicts through proper training.
- Create inter-generational mentoring programs.
- Reward and recognize both individuals and teams for exceptional behaviors.
- Tune into employees personal lives: people take care of what affects them the most before anything else.
- Recognize and respect what people value the most.
- Be flexible and family supportive to your people.

The Challenges Ahead

It is evident that the workforce is going through a metamorphosis. The portrait of the typical American is changing, as is the entire picture of the workforce. *Chal-*

lenges occurring today are simply indicators of what you will be faced with in the future. As the labor pool shrinks and becomes increasingly female, multi-ethnic, older, and certainly not wiser educationally, businesses will have to become more flexible and better at handling these changes. It is not a matter of social justice, but one of filling the jobs that are available.

Because these changes are happening so rapidly, corporate executives, managers, and small business owners will find it difficult to adjust and find workable solutions. Management philosophies developed in the 1930s through the 1970s are still being applied today to solve problems these changes create. Yesterday's policies, procedures, and practices have become obsolete with today's workforce. *How you managed in the past simply won't work in the next century.*

Management must look at how work itself is structured, and how this effects serving the customer. This needs to be done in terms of the different needs of individual workers. What motivated and challenged the workers of the industrial era is far different than what motivates the current breed of American workers in the information age. More choices need to be created, as people have different expectations. More options need to be made available as people have different needs.

The challenge for management today is to embrace the changes that are happening, rather than fight them. More specifically, the key is to become flexible in handling our wide diversity of workers, and find unique ways to manage this diversity. The new workers will not fit the current mold. *The time has come for management to change.*

If your business is to become known as a superior service organization, you will have do things differently. You must get better at recruiting and hiring, training people to give great service, recognize and reward them for their contributions, recognize and support them in whatever ways they are different, and support people in their lives outside of work.

2

Management's New Role

"What we call the beginning is often the end
And to make an end is to make a beginning.
The end is where we start from."

T.S. Eliot

The changes in the workforce have dramatically altered the role of management today and its role will continue to evolve well into the 21st Century. As managers or owners, we need to learn to discard old methods and accept the new concepts. Today's workforce doesn't have the same wants, needs, or concerns that workers did in the '30s, or '60s or even the '80s. People don't respond to the same motivators and methods that worked in the past. Directing, controlling, and giving orders to people will not motivate them to achieve outstanding service. In today's workplace, control has to be shared. People want to become partners in reaching an organization's goals.

This is not to say that today's workplace should be out of control, with no direction. Chapter five will show how critical it is to control standards of service and employee behaviors towards customers. Having certain policies and rules in place are critical. Management now has to create the type of atmosphere where people are motivated to direct and control their own behaviors and outputs, through involvement, participation, teamwork, and empowerment.

Let's look at management's new role, and what that role is in motivating the changing workforce to achieve outstanding service and performance. These are the roles, that a manager as an enabler and leader must undertake to be successful now and into the 21st Century.

Role Model

There is an old saying in the Yukon, *"The speed of the leader is the speed of the pack."* Leaders always set the tone and pace. Many of the true service superstar companies have shining examples of top people at the helm who "walk the talk." They are great examples of role models whose ideals, values, and behaviors are emulated by those who work for them. Such examples include: Horst Schultze of the Ritz Carlton Hotel Company, Bill Marriott Jr. of the Marriott Corporation, Jan Carlzon of Scandinavian Airlines, and Fred Smith of Federal Express.

As a leader, you need to role model the behaviors that you want your employees to exhibit. *"Do as I say, but not as I do"* just won't work anymore. If you want people to be in on time and work hard, then *you* need to be in on time and work hard. If you want employees to treat co-workers and customers with care and concern, then you need to treat employees and customers the same way.

Employees spend a lot of time watching and listening to what their supervisors and managers do and say. They listen to their dialogues with others and overhear their phone conversations. Employees want to know how managers treat people, including customers, suppliers, and their families. If they see them lying, cheating, or stealing, they may decide this type of behavior is acceptable for them. If these behaviors conflict with their values, then they just may decide to find employment elsewhere.

Employees are greatly affected by bosses who are critical, moody, have tantrums, or use threats. Using abusive or obscene language, shouting, verbal put-downs, insults, and lying can only result in low employee morale, high absenteeism, and turnover. As finding qualified individuals becomes increasingly difficult, professional respect and courtesy can do a lot to shut a "revolving door."

Managers and supervisors who are positive and upbeat will dramatically impact their people's productivity and service level. Those who model high moral values, with unimpeachable honesty and integrity, will gain their employees' respect, trust and commitment.

Motivator

Bill Hewlett, the founder of Hewlett-Packard once said, "Men and women want to do a good job, and if they are provided the proper environment, they will do so." Our priority is to create a motivating, positive, open environment; an environment that stimulates people to give their very best to serve the customer.

A good motivator realizes that not everyone will thrive in this environment. With such a diverse workforce, some people are not self-starters and may need more direction. It is up to you as the manager to know what motivates each individual. Get to know each person. Learn which buttons to push to bring out their true potential.

As a motivator, you have to exhibit some exceptional people skills and behaviors towards your employees. You have to be able to inspire, excite, and influence others. You have to know when to encourage, when to correct, and when to praise. You must learn when to be supportive, nurturing, and give counsel. At the same time, you must refuse to accept anything less than good performance. You have to do all this, with many different people and personalities. It takes a tremendous amount of forethought, insight, and ability.

No matter how you may feel internally you must be enthusiastic. Enthusiasm is infectious. It overcomes stress and apathy. Enthusiasm can produce success with people when you think it's impossible. Recently, a general manager in one of my seminars stated, "Remember the last four letters of the word enthusiasm as an acronym (I.A.S.M.) which means: I Am Sold Myself." He said, *"If you can't sell yourself on what you're doing each day, then you can't expect to sell anyone else, or lead them."*

Assuming you have hired the best and most capable people, your job as a motivator is to get employees to do what you want during the time they are on the job. That means serving your customers, whether they are external or internal. If they are not performing, your job is to find out why and help correct the situation.

Employees can only perform if they know exactly what their roles are, have clear performance standards, and have all the necessary tools to perform their job properly. If they don't have what they need, your efforts to motivate are wasted. Make sure they have everything they need. If you are not a top level manager, then go to the top and fight for the things they need.

If their work performance is up to pre-set standards, or is exceptional, your job as a motivator is to reinforce, praise, and thank them. Be sure they get the bonuses, recognition, and rewards they deserve for giving excellent service.

Communicator

The old ways of management stem from the early 1900s. It was a system where owners and managers made all the rules and decisions in secrecy and isolation. The main decision makers were the older, White American male, and no one ever questioned their authority. Everyone went along with the program, or they were fired. It was "my way or the highway."

With the changing workforce, turnover is expensive and time consuming. Emphasis must be placed on collaboration and information sharing. Instead of relying on rules and edicts, your focus must be on productive and profitable outcomes. Communication should be open and unguarded in all directions.

Today's employees want to know why or how decisions from the top affect them. They want to know where the organization is going, and how it will change their lives. Workers want to know how the organization is doing, both the good and the bad. They need to feel that this is their organization, and that their opinions and feelings are being heard and considered.

When you communicate with your people frankly and openly, it prevents the growth of the grapevine. When you hear rumors and gossip, there is a very simple way to eliminate them: be truthful. Let employees know whenever they have questions about a rumor that they can come directly to you or another manager. Then you need to give them the real facts, or tell them when they will know (if the information is not for public disclosure yet).

The faster you get information out to everyone, the quicker the rumors will be squashed. Be sure your management team does the same. Once you have gained workers' trust through consistent honesty, then you will have created an open climate, where your people can thrive.

One idea that is quite effective is to let the responsibility of communication throughout your organization fall to one department or team. They can take the information from top management, create the best medium or method to get the message across, and deliver the communication along the best channels. Whatever medium is chosen, the message must be consistent every time it is heard. Allow feedback to come back up the channel or to that department. This is critical to understanding employees' reactions to the information being sent.

Be sure they get the information exactly, and it is delivered very clearly so there are no misunderstandings. Don't send conflicting or multiple messages. Remember that clear, open and honest communication enables people to "buy-in," and that is what you want.

Managers who communicate effectively have the ability to make themselves easily understood by their peers and the front line. They are able to speak at everyone's individual level. Whether speaking to the team, or one-on-one with an individual, everyone knows what the message is. They aren't hypocritical, and they don't send mixed messages.

Effective managers are skilled listeners. They physically show they are listening by their body language and facial expressions. They give their undivided attention to show they are truly interested. They focus in on the speaker.

They listen for both content and meaning; they are able to understand inferred messages.

The ability to effectively communicate is not automatic. In any organization it takes hard work and practice. The end results greatly outweigh the time and effort spent.

If you ignore the importance of communications, it's much like the person who ignores putting oil in the car engine. The car will run for awhile with no negative outward signs. So too, your organization will run for awhile with no negative outward signs, but eventually it will begin to burn up on the inside.

Coach and Mentor

The German philosopher Goethe once said, "Human relations means treating people as if they were what they ought to be, and then you help them to become what they are capable of being." When you treat workers as if you expect them to exhibit exceptional skills and behavior, you help them to achieve superior performance. Not only are you improving the quality of individuals and their service performance, but you are also creating a positive long-term working relationship with those employees.

Often, this Pygmalion effect or self-fulfilling prophecy is a factor that affects employee performance. If you treat employees as if you expect them to fail, they will. If you don't expect them to achieve high standards, they won't. Many young workers and those that arrive from other countries claim this is the way they are often treated in the workplace. They tell us in surveys because of their differences, youth and inexperience, they are often treated as misfits or slackards.

If you treat employees as if they will succeed, then they will. If you expect them to achieve high standards then they will. If you treat them as winners, that is what you will get.

As a coach, mentor, and developer of your employees, there are certain roles you must fulfill that are critical to your people achieving success. These include:

1. Clarify the role of the individual.
2. Clarify individual and team performance goals.
3. Teach employees the skills and behaviors needed.
4. Reinforce the positive performance.
5. Correct areas needing improvement through feedback.
6. Create opportunities for personal development and growth.
7. Help employees achieve their personal goals.
8. Help create a career path.
9. Model positive behaviors.

Unfortunately, many supervisors and managers are not accustom to these roles, or feel they don't have time to undertake them. They spend a lot of their time solving problems, making decisions, and giving orders. Some feel there is no return on the investment of their time to coach and mentor those who are not exceptional performers. The reality is that there is a tremendous payback in improved service, performance, loyalty, and commitment.

The coaching and mentoring relationship just doesn't happen. It starts with you. If you are to be successful at it, you need to sit down with the employee on a frequent basis and talk. All good relationships take time.

Let's face it. There are also going to be times when an employee doesn't respond to the corrective feedback you have given. Performance is less than the pre-set standards, or the employee is breaking one of the house rules. You will need more than just a short discussion to correct the situation. You need to have a formal coaching session. Here are some steps that will help you to coach your people more effectively, with the main outcome being improved performance:

1. Observe or analyze the insufficient performance.

   The only way you can know if performance is not acceptable is to observe it, observe the results of it, or collect data from someone else who did. You need to know what behavior, output, or results were below standard, and be able to prove it.

2. Show specific examples of the lack of performance.

   Some employees will either deny there is a problem, or divorce themselves from it. With the necessary proof, whether it be statistics, charts, or other documented evidence, you can easily show them where there is a problem and their involvement.

3. Explain what has to change for performance (or service) to improve.

   Let them know exactly the expected outcomes. Agree upon the solution, and together create a step-by-step action plan. Set a deadline date for you to meet and discuss their progress. Then if necessary, set another meeting for a further progress report.

4. Check-up to see if there is improvement along the way.

   If there is, then praise and encourage them. Thank them for making the efforts. Let them know it hasn't gone unnoticed. After they have accomplished the change, be sure they don't return to their old ways.

5. Have a plan in place, if there is no improvement.

6. Implement the plan.

   If you allow non-performance to continue, it will soon affect other employees. The bad employees can run off some of the good ones, and, you never know how many customers they are running off.

   In surveying managers in my seminars, they all agree that you can't let it go on very long. Most seem to agree that you should not have to sit down with a person more than two or three times to change behavior or improve performance. At some point, you must either transfer the employee or terminate the relationship.

Supporter/Provider

In the early 1980s, when Jan Carlzon created his success story at Scandinavian Airlines, he took the company from a loss of $8 million to a gain of $71 million in a little over a year. One of the reasons for his success was that he told managers their role was to become a supporter and provider of the front line. He reasoned that if you give people all that they need to serve the customer, they will be successful in satisfying them. He was right on target with his idea.

If you support and provide your staff with all the information, resources, tools, and equipment they need to do their job, then you have eliminated many of the reasons for not performing.

Ask questions such as: What can I do to help your performance, or to make you more productive? What can I do for you that will help you give better quality, or reduce the number of mistakes?

Too many organizations send out the message: we only care about you while you are at work; your personal life is your business. The attitude is that if people take the time to help each other, they are somehow stealing time or being unproductive. What happens in your employees' personal lives directly affects what happens to your customers. Helping them to make the correct decisions can only pay off with increased employee loyalty and commitment. They may not be as productive in the short term but in the long term, you will reap the benefits. People don't forget when you have taken the time and energy to help get them through the rough times in their lives.

Support your staff with difficult personal decisions and family problems in any way you can. Show your people empathy. Let them know that you understand what they are going through, and that you understand their feelings and emotions. Just knowing that you realize certain situations are taking place at home and are behind them, can go a long way towards have a very dedicated employee.

Managers in the next twenty years will be a different breed, unlike any that has gone before. With the demands of global competition, new technology, and customer expectations, you and your employees will be forced to give maximum performance and total quality service. And you, as a leader in this new era must enable this evolving workforce to achieve their peak performance to satisfy your customers.

Quick Chapter Tips

1. The old methods of managing won't work with today's new breed of workers. Just as the workforce is changing, you must change.

2. A manager must lead by example. It's critical to be a role model to your employees. Always model the behaviors you want them to exhibit.

3. Being a good motivator is a difficult task and can't be taken lightly. You have to work with many different personalities who have different wants and needs.

4. Learn to manage each person as an individual. Find out what motivates each one.

5. Keep the channels of communication open in all directions. Employees need to know where they fit in. They want to be told how decisions affect their lives.

6. Treat your employees as if they are the best they can be. Expect the most from them, and you will get it.

7. Become a coach and mentor to your staff. Take time to ensure they are performing to standards. If they aren't, find out how to help them achieve those standards.

8. Don't keep non-performing employees. They will only run off the good employees, and your customers.

9. Provide your people with all the tools they need to get the job done. If they don't have everything they need, then do whatever it takes to get it for them.

10. Support your staff with personal decisions and problems. Showing them empathy and that you are behind them will go a long way towards having dedicated employees.

3

Managing and Motivating the Next Generation

It's often said that kids today aren't what they used to be. Is this new generation of teenagers and twenty plus adults really so different than previous generations; and if so, what impact are they having on your workplace?

Let's look at some trends that have begun to emerge from this young generation, commonly known as "Generation X," "baby busters," and "Yiffies" (young, individualistic, freedom-minded, and few).

Extensive research has been done by U.C.L.A.'s Higher Education Research Institute on young people. They issue a report annually, entitled "The American Freshman: National Norms for Fall," that illustrates the values, attitudes, and beliefs of thousands of college freshman across the country. These yearly profiles have also been compiled into a book entitled, *The American Freshman: Twenty Year Trends* (Dey, Astin, & Korn, 1991). Spanning from 1966 to 1990, the compiled data paints an extensive portrait of how young people have changed over the years to where they are today. Here are some trends that have emerged. Keep in mind, there are many exceptions to the rule. No generation is homogeneous in its values and attitudes.

Characteristics

Few in Numbers

As a result of our workforce growing at the slowest rate since the 1930s, skilled and educated Yiffies realize the numbers are on their side. They see themselves as very marketable commodities in the workforce. They are critically needed and in short supply. They feel they can be patient when choosing a job. Consequently, many have become highly competitive at getting what they want.

Keep Options Open

The baby busters or Yiffies, as a whole, take longer to make job decisions. Often commitments don't last. Part of the reason is that they want to keep their options open. The grass always seems greener somewhere else.

Yiffies are always looking to upgrade their work and out-of-work situations. In order to upgrade their careers, they tend to leave a job at the hint of a better position. This baffles and frustrates their baby boomer managers. Boomers are accustomed to giving two weeks to a month's notice prior to leaving.

One owner of an engineering firm related an experience to me about hiring a Yiffie. He was happy to find the "ideal candidate" for a position within his practice because of a shortage of engineering students coming out of college. He had interviewed over ten people before offering her the position.

The young lady was just out of graduate school with an M.B.A., and an engineering degree. She agreed to begin work in thirty days, but first she wanted to take care of some personal matters. The morning she was to begin, she called him and told him that she had taken another job for more money. He said from the sound of her voice, it seemed as if it were to her, a routine decision. He couldn't understand how she could be so "thoughtless and cold." She really had put him in a bind.

The loyalty and commitment to the workplace previous generations had is a thing of the past. They watched their grandparents do everything perfectly right only to get a gold watch and collect a pension upon retirement. Their parents' dedication to the company only seemed to result in job losses because of lay-offs, mergers, and acquisitions. This generation sees no good reason for commitment. "Baby busters may be the first group since World War II to enter business knowing that the days of the company man—who could climb through the ranks of one corporation—are finished" (Samon, 1990, p. 68).

Young and Flexible

One of their key strengths is the fact that they are young. This enables Yiffies or Generation X'ers to take jobs where physical work or standing all day is a requirement. They normally have high energy levels and can handle stress well. Many are filled with innocent enthusiasm. Depending on the job requirements, their youth enables them to easily switch gears and they are willing to try new tasks. In fact, they like the challenge that comes with new situations. Generations X'ers are bored with repetitive tasks.

Selfishness

This is the first generation to spend considerable time in day care centers. They became independent at a young age. The X'ers have been weaned on MTV, high-tech, video games, and computers. They've had a lot of free time after school as both (if they had two) of their baby boom generation parents worked. Many were latchkey children, and this helped them become very freedom-minded, individualistic, and self absorbed, bordering on selfish.

"The latchkey experience has undoubtedly made these children more independent and self sufficient at an earlier age than previous generations. For some, depending on their own resources may have even started before the traditional peer pressure associated with elementary school" (Dunn, 1993, p. 21).

This has enabled Generation X'ers to work very well by themselves in the workplace. They are self-directed and often have great initiative for a new challenge. However, many are not adept, early on, at working in teams. With team building training, they can easily assimilate, and they enjoy working with peers.

Stay at Home Longer

This generation seems to do things at a much later age than their parents did. They graduate from college later, stay at home longer, and marry much later. In 1992, 13.2 million people 18 to 24 years of age were living with their parents. That's over two million more than in 1970 (Dunn, 1993).

Some of this is due to the high cost of living. Contrary to the baby boomers, who couldn't wait to leave home when they became adults, this generation saves their money so they can live better when they do leave. Or, perhaps they want to finish their education before moving out. Some just want to delay the time when they are on their own because they spent so much time alone as a child.

Crave Attention

Many of the X'ers' parents were very busy in the morning getting ready for work. At night, their parents were often too tired to have any meaningful, quality time with them. At school, classes were overcrowded. It was hard for the X'ers to get noticed. As adults, they still have a great need to be noticed. As a result, they seek that attention in the workplace.

Some managers have complained to me about their young workers' bizarre behaviors that were hard to understand. I tell them to sit down with the employee when this happens and have a coaching session. Describe the exact behavior to the person, and ask why they are exhibiting it. Almost all the answers will revolve around one reason: gaining attention. Young workers are insecure. They are afraid nobody will know they exist.

Propensity for Fun

This generation was entertained by Big Bird and Company from Sesame Street. Many spent time after school entertaining themselves, so it's only natural that a good time, whether it be at work, school, or home is a priority. They don't take work seriously like their baby boomer parents did. They disdain the workaholic, slave-to-the-job mentality of their parents and Yuppies in general. Work is only a means to an end: money, fun, and leisure are their priorities. Many owners and managers I've spoken to voice the same opinion: this group doesn't work very hard. Those that hire the pre-twenty year olds for their restaurant or retail outlets say they have to really keep an eye on them to get them to be productive. Young employees spend a lot of time chatting and laughing with young co-workers. Many customers complain that they can't get clerks to wait on them because they are too busy wasting time.

Don't Respect the Boss

This group hasn't had any experience with the military, unless it was their choice. Authority figures and bosses are an anomaly to them. Their parents often weren't around enough to tell them what to do or were too soft with their discipline. They don't like to take orders. They always question why when they are told to do something.

Baby boomer managers feel their behaviors border on disrespectful because X'ers tend to work around their managers, or skip over them and go directly to the top.

One supervisor in a credit union shared with me how some of his young employees would go directly to his manager when they had an important request. No matter how many times they discussed it, he could not change the situation. The employees told him they weren't disrespectful, but they just wanted to interact with higher management, because it was good for their career. They also thought their direct input could make changes faster.

Negative View of the World

It is estimated that by the time this group became eighteen years old, they had watched over 22,000 hours of TV (Dunn, 1993), and as a result, witnessed thousands of murders and acts of violence. In addition, their gloomy view of the world was shaped by numerous negative events they have witnessed. Events such as the Persian Gulf War, escalating crime, riots, nuclear threat, and greater pollution have helped mold their views.

This is a generation that grew up with parents who practiced birth control and abortion. Their parents were most concerned about making it in the world. This seems to have sent out a negative message to X'ers about their value and worth.

About 40% of X'ers are products of divorce, and were brought up in single parent homes. This is the highest divorce rate in the world (Dunn, 1993). The emotional upheaval and conflict caused by divorce helped shape their view of the family and the world.

Unrealistic and Materialistic Views

Whether it be from watching TV, or from being given too much by their guilt-ridden, never-home parents, the baby busters have come to expect a whole lot for nothing. Their grandparents also contributed to this by lavishly awarding them with gifts and money. Their motto could almost be: "I exist, therefore I get." They have a strong propensity for instant gratification. They want it all, and they want it fast.

In many conversations with X'ers, I found their favorite TV programs to be soap operas. They would also like their world to be filled with the same good looking people, dressed in the latest fashions with lots of money and prestige. Plus, they never have to work hard.

It is not uncommon for them to get out of high school and expect to be paid well for minimal skills. Many disdain minimum wage jobs at fast food chains; the ones that they refer to as "McJobs." Young college graduates look to start at high paying positions with power and perks. They have little patience for paying their dues or working their way up.

They do feel the need to have material things and gadgets, yet they reject the materialistic consumption of the Yuppies. The X'ers feel making money is not as important as experiencing life. To be a workaholic is to have no life. Consequently, a paradox exists between how they view life, and what they think they need from it.

Interestingly, the student surveys in *The American Freshman* have shown a dramatic increase of students who want to get masters' and doctoral degrees. It is at an all time high (Dey, Astin, & Korn, 1991). One explanation may be that they think only an advanced degree will start them at a high paying job. It also reflects their need for money and status.

The freshman data also showed a strong increase in the phrase wanting to be "very well-off financially." In 1970, the endorsement of this value was at 39.1%. In 1987, it jumped to a record high of 76% of students endorsing this value. During the same time period, there is a dramatic decline of "developing a meaningful philosophy of life," and a prolonged decline in an interest of involvement with altruistic activities (Dey, Astin, & Korn, 1991).

The Keys to Managing Them

Is there hope, or are they a lost generation? Should owners and managers be worried about hiring them? Although some of their characteristics exasperate both the baby boomers and radio generation (pre 1944), the answers are much more positive than many managers and owners would expect. With the right management and motivating techniques, this energetic, creative, enthusiastic generation is ready to contribute, and has much to offer. Many companies have been highly successful in employing them.

Apple Computer is one leader in hiring and managing Generation X'ers. One of the reasons for their success is that, "The Apple culture, while rigorous, also rewards employees in precisely the way management experts say young people need to be rewarded" (Doyle, 1993, p. 83). Apple is dedicated to developing each individual person. Employees are given a six week sabbatical every five years where they reassess their career path goals and make changes, if needed. Contrary to what one may think, Apple has an incredibly low turnover rate.

Patagonia, a manufacturer of various types of products for active people, employs a workforce where 40% are under thirty years of age. Young workers like Patagonia's work environment. One of the attractions is that there are no walls, only open work areas. Employees are able to choose flexi-scheduling around a core set of hours. They have the option to work part of the day at home. People can take an unpaid work leave of up to four months per year. Employees are paid about 10-20% higher than similar companies. In addition, they empower their people to take risks, create new work processes, and solve problems (Solomon, 1992).

Texas Instruments uses education and training as an incentive to keep younger people. Employees are reimbursed 100% for pursuing an advanced degree. Education and training are used as a basis for promotions and pay raises.

The company has changed its hourly compensation system for young employees. It used to be based upon seniority. Now the system is based on overall performance, with seniority being a minor factor (Solomon, 1992).

The following methods are particularly productive for managing people under age thirty. They can be applied to employees of all ages.

Accept Them

The first thing to remember is that this the next generation. They will not go away and *are here to stay*. Accept them and learn to work with them rather than fight them. It's a lot easier. Showing that you don't like them only creates conflicts and turnover. Don't refer to this generation in negative terms, or use expressions such as "you people," or "your generation." Eliminate expressions such as "When I was your age . . ."

Use Love and Caring

This is a group that needs to be shown that you truly care about them as a person. They often did not get this from their own parents. They need to know that they matter. Talking about how you care about them or appreciate the job they are doing just doesn't get it. To them talk is cheap. They say, "show me how much you care or appreciate me." So, a key to motivating them is to *show* you care or appreciate them. But, be careful. *They hate anything that smacks of phoniness and can spot it a mile away.*

Don't Baby Them

Generation X'ers want the care and concern, yet don't want to be babied. They want you to guide them, but also want to be seen as independent and self starters. It's no wonder that managers get confused when managing this generation! Don't baby them, but do be a surrogate parent to them in the beginning. If it's their first job, they will be nervous and want you there in case they need you.

They don't want anyone to see them being babied as it conflicts with their independence and embarrasses them. At the same time, they love the strokes. Once you have proven yourself as a caring manager, the battle is over, as long as you manage in a manner that continually shows you care.

If you treat them like children, that's exactly what you will get. If you want them to act like adults, then *talk to them adult to adult, not parent to child.*

Hands Off, but Be There

Give them some freedom and independence. This may seem a bit of a paradox as this group likes a lot of inter-action with their manager. At the same time, they are cynical toward bosses. You can accomplish this by giving them some autonomy and responsibility, but also be sure to take the time to chat with them. Be there enough to ensure success during those first critical days and weeks. Empower them to make decisions, but let them know how far they can go before consulting you.

Remember, this is a group that thrives on working by themselves. This may be due to the many hours spent alone. They get a tremendous amount of satisfaction by what they create, analyze, and solve.

Ask, Ask, Ask

Another key to managing Generation X'ers is what I call, "Management By Asking Questions." The #1 rule of asking questions is: don't ask unless you have time to listen to the answers. The #2 rule of asking questions is: don't ask them unless you are willing to implement the changes based on those answers. The third rule is: when in doubt, refer to rules #1 and #2.

Asking lots of questions and implementing solutions based on those answers does three things with this generation. First, it shows that you value and respect their opinion. Second, it gets them involved and participating in decisions, which they love. X'ers take to empowerment very well. Third, it builds loyalty and commitment.

Effective Questions to Ask Young Workers

1. What do I do that you would like me to do more of?
2. What would you like me to do that I don't do?
3. If you could change one other thing about me, what would it be?
4. What is the best way for me to be helpful and supportive to you?
5. When we have a problem or disagreement, what is the best way for us to discuss it?
6. What kind of feedback is most helpful to you?
7. How do you know when you are doing a good job?
8. What do you need to do a better job (be more productive, give better service)?
9. How do you like to be rewarded and recognized for exceptional work?
10. Have you ever thought about quitting? Why?

Discuss Your Methods

Next, explain to them how you like to manage, communicate with them, and evaluate them. One method I found to be very helpful is to determine what is the best way to discuss a problem or conflict with them. Let's face it: there will be times when you just disagree. By discussing matters ahead of time, you gain a lot of insight. You'll know what will or won't work.

Ask what they liked or disliked about the way they were treated by previous managers, owners, or teachers. Tell them how your methods compare. This is good not only as an interview question, but one that is effective in the first few weeks of employment. It gives you a clue about which buttons of their's to push or not to push.

Train and Orient

When Generation X'ers first come to work for you, do as much training and orientation as you feel is necessary for them to be effective immediately. Meet with them after day one, week one, month one, quarterly, and at the end of the year. You need to know if they are having problems, and where they need help. You also need to ask if they have thought about quitting, or if they are happy with their jobs. In addition, find out what they need to do their jobs better, or how you can help them be more effective. Empower them to make their jobs more effective and productive. This also helps you to get to know them individually. The greatest management riddle in the world is how to treat each person as an individual, but yet be fair and consistent with everyone. This is a group that demands fairness.

Set Specific Standards

Next, you must communicate what you want. This means *it is critical to write out the specific standards of behavior, responsibilities, and policies you expect.* Unless clear standards are written out and communicated, what you want will not happen. If you are not explicit about the behaviors you want, any behavior will do. This generation is not irresponsible. Many just haven't been taught enough about responsibility.

When something goes wrong, it is important not to let it slide by. It needs to be discussed. Let them know when the behavior is unacceptable, and that it won't be tolerated.

If you ignore negative behavior, it will happen again and usually very soon. There is a testing period, where young people will try to learn how far they can push the rules, or see what they can get away with. But, don't overreact any more than you would with anyone else. This is a normal response for boomer managers as we often do it with our own children. We think because the employee is young that we have to break them in hard, or "ride herd" on them. This management technique will only create a revolving door syndrome.

X'ers are good at frowning, rolling their eyes back, or making subtle noises. "They express distaste or irritation through melodramatic sighs, or ignore your attempts to get their attention by hanging on to a personal call" (Samon, 1990, p. 69).

These behaviors can't be tolerated. One owner of a chain of retail outlets that I have consulted with lets his people know, "I am not your parents, and this is not school. This is a business, and we respect each other. Your behavior is unacceptable when you . . ., and you can leave if it doesn't change."

Be consistent in what you expect. Don't lower your standards and don't have different standards for different people. Young people already view the world as being unfair.

At the same time, learn to be flexible when necessary. Offering young people more options and choices in such areas as scheduling and benefits is very motivating to them. Matching their job to their skills and interest is also a powerful motivator.

Use Written Contracts

If a young person is not cooperating, or not following the standards set, then try something else. Try using written agreements and contracts. They are used to doing this with their parents and teachers. This also works well when you want them to accomplish a particular task or goal.

Here are some guidelines when you use a written contract:

1. Clearly explain the service behavior, or goal you want accomplished. Have them explain it back to you, in their own words, so both of you are clear on what is expected. Then put the standards expected down on paper and have them sign off on it.

2. Give them a specific date when it must be accomplished. A goal is just a wish unless it is written down. Young people are terrific at procrastinating because they are not used to setting goals.

3. Examine their improvement. On certain pre-determined dates, sit down and discuss their progress. If they know they have mini-deadlines, they will keep working toward their goal.

4. Explain to them how they will be appraised. You want to let them know exactly what you will be looking for, and how they will be judged. If done properly, this eliminates a lot of the fear, and they are more apt to do a better job.

5. If they do an exceptional job, reward and recognize them accordingly. If you have evaluated their progress at the mini-deadlines, they will have succeeded. If, for any reason, they don't succeed, have a plan in place to deal with the failure.

Show Them What's in it for Them

You can't motivate them by telling them what they are doing is for the good of the organization. That just doesn't fly. You have to explain what the benefits are for them or the customer.

Just as it was important in school to know why they should learn something, it is equally important to explain why they need to learn a particular skill or how to perform a task. By letting them know why it is important in their career, they will forge ahead with enthusiasm and energy. It's imperative to them that the things they are learning in their job or career are going to make a difference further down the road. It has to make them a hotter commodity in the job marketplace.

Share Company Information

Share as much information as you can about your company. Managers and owners are often shocked at suggestions I make in my seminars about sharing information on the balance sheet and the bottom line. But this shock quickly disappears, when we ask for a show of hands and comments from those that have discovered that it works. This generation tells us they want to see the big picture. They want to know where they fit into the scheme of things.

Support Them Outside of Work

Show your support for their difficult personal situations. Remember: people pay attention to what hurts them the most emotionally. This is a difficult time for young people. As one owner of a chain of fast food restaurants told me, "They are hormones in uniform." Many times they don't have anyone that will listen. Take the time to listen, and you will be rewarded with higher dedication on their part. You don't have to get involved but do show that you care.

Make Work Fun

Learn to make work as much fun as possible. Sales contests and games work very well with this group. Have friendly competition between individual or teams for a predetermined service goal. Spotlight the winners on a bulletin board or display case. Put their photos up where customers can see them. Most young workers like the attention and recognition. If you are not sure that they will like it, ask them.

One fun award I developed for a retail chain that hired very young workers was an award called the "Customer Maniac of the Month." The award winner wore a button with those words on it, along with their name. The customers frequently asked them about the award, and how they got it. The employees loved the attention as they got an opportunity to talk about themselves.

Give Proper Feedback

X'ers want to know how they are doing. They crave feedback. They are used to instant feedback from the computer games they played while growing up. They want to know both the good and the bad. They want you to tell them frequently what they are doing right, and what they are doing wrong.

Learn the proper way to give feedback to this group (see Chapter Nine). Again, don't talk down to them as a parent correcting a child. Concentrate on the behavior you actually saw, or of which you saw the result.

Guard your choice of words. Stay away from words such as "immature," "childish," or, "unprofessional." These words are emotional and explosive and only make the situation worse. Let them know what they are doing wrong, why it bothers you, and how you would like them to change it. And, one more thing: always ask, "How can I help?"

Reward and Recognize

The last area critical to managing Generation X'ers is to reward and recognize them for exceptional behavior. I don't believe in rewarding people who are just doing the minimum. I feel the most should go to the best. If people go above and beyond what is required, and you want them to continue to do so, be sure to recognize it in words or action, and reward it in some way.

With young people, we find it's best to reward them with things that are important to them at that particular moment. The more you know about each Yiffie, the better you can manage and motivate them. Therefore, you have to ask! One person may prefer concert tickets, and another may want to go to a sporting event.

This group loves to be rewarded with awards that are "in" at the moment. As consummate shoppers, they know what is in. They don't respond to the rewards of the two previous generations. Since they are into having fun, any kind of award that is fun, or related to their free time, outdoors, or leisure will often work. Tie it into their lifestyles whenever possible.

This generation has evolved in dramatically different ways from those who came before them. Those that make changes in their management style for a different kind of young worker will be the ones who will have less turnover and fewer hiring setbacks. Service gaps that occur from being shorthanded will be reduced. This is the workforce of tomorrow, and the organizations that can manage them well will be the ones who stay a step ahead of the competition.

Quick Chapter Tips

1. Generation X'ers (or baby busters, Yiffies) are fewer in number than the baby boomers that preceded them. As a result, they are in demand in the workplace, and they know it. They keep their employment options open, are less loyal, and change jobs frequently.

2. This generation spent a great deal of time home alone and were latchkey children. As a result, they are independent, and at the same time crave attention and love. They live at home longer than previous generations.

3. Having fun in the workplace and after work is of primary importance to X'ers.

4. Being the boss doesn't guarantee respect from X'ers. They will often question your decisions and won't hesitate to go above your head to resolve a matter.

5. Generation X'ers generally have a negative view of the world, and tend to be cynical.

6. The key to managing this generation is to accept them. Don't treat them as outcasts. Show X'ers that you genuinely care about them and their success.

7. Make sure you are there when they need you, but don't baby X'ers, especially in front of others.

8. Generation X'ers crave having their opinion valued by their superiors. Ask a lot of questions to show that you care and want their involvement. At the same time, answer their questions and share information. They want to know where they fit in.

9. If Generation X'ers don't know what is expected of them, then any behavior will do. Set very high standards, train X'ers for those standards, and accept nothing less from them.

10. X'ers are used to having written contracts with their parents and teachers. You can use written contracts with them to improve job performance and productivity.

11. Take advantage of their propensity for fun. Use contests and games to motivate them. Reward and recognize X'ers with awards and feedback that are meaningful to them.

12. Take an interest in their personal lives. X'ers often bring their problems with them to work. Support them in any way you can. By letting them know you are concerned, you'll be rewarded with their loyalty and commitment.

How to Recruit and Hire with a Changing Workforce

As the workforce continues to age, and there are less people entering the workforce, it will become increasingly difficult to find good people. *Your greatest challenge will be to match job requirements and service skills to the qualifications of the people available.* Competition will increase for the best workers. Preventing costly turnover will become one of your highest priorities. Consequently, you will have to get better at recruiting, interviewing, assessing, hiring, training, and motivating employees.

Recruiting the Changing Workforce

The old traditional ways of finding good service employees may not work with today's very different workforce. You have to be creative, innovative, and learn to think "outside the box." *Be proactive.* That means, always be recruiting! You can't wait until you have openings before you begin looking.

Here are some good recruiting sources to explore:

Recruitment Agencies

In the past, recruitment agencies were relatively expensive and concentrated mainly on finding top management. Some of the newer recruitment agencies are now involved in finding people for hard to fill front line or basic supervisory positions. They may charge less than the traditional agencies. When cost is a factor, look for the newer ones, as they tend to be less expensive.

Don't overlook your own state employment agency. They are a good source for blue collar workers. Many state employment agencies now have many white collar professionals and managers who are readily available.

Temporary Agencies

"Temp" agencies are a good source, and sometimes they are overlooked. Temp workers cost more to employ than if you hire people on your own. Our recent surveys have shown that more and more companies who hire blue-collar workers are making use of these services. Some businesses, because of the nature of their physical work, have great difficulty in getting anyone to do the job. Applicants feel, for the amount of money that they are being paid, they would rather be on welfare. Some of these companies use temporary agencies exclusively for all their hiring. They often enter into an agreement with the agency where after two months, if the employee does a good job, the company can hire them permanently.

Many agencies foot the bill for workers compensation benefits. This is a real savings, and a good reason to use temps. Temporary agencies also take care of all the paperwork and the payroll. An added advantage is that screening of the applicant is already done for you, and you don't have to go through the hiring process. So, temps are time savers as well.

Advertising

Think about the advertising you have done in the past. Has it worked? Are you getting the quality of service people that you need? If not, then consider changing your methods. For example, many employers advertise traditionally in the classified section of the Sunday newspapers. Try different sections on different days.

One owner of a tire dealership knows that his technicians all read the sports section first, and certainly on Saturday for the weekend games. He places his advertisements on page two of this section because he knows they will always turn to this page as it lists the T.V. schedule for games. He gets a great response.

Try alternative newspapers other than the major ones in your city. The smaller, local newspapers are found on racks outside stores in shopping centers. Your ad will stand out more because there are less ads competing with one another. In addition, the people applying will be closer to home so they won't leave the job because they have a long commute.

Be sure your ad stands out from the others. It should be large and unique. Make it sincere and factual, stating the benefits of working for your service organization. Let it be warm and personal, showing that you are a humane organization. Have the ad communicate the service values of your business. Be sure that your wording doesn't discriminate against any group.

Billboard advertising has been around for many years and has a reasonable success rate, depending on the location and the ad itself. One ingenious owner of a small manufacturing company got the idea of creating his own portable billboard. He placed it inside the back of his truck. The billboard was tent shaped and had the same ad on both sides. It listed the benefits of working for him, along with a phone number. His young son, who just got his drivers license, was more than willing to drive around and advertise. The owner kept watching the newspaper for any plant closings and would send his son out to drive around at the beginning and end of the work day. He also did this at other plants where he heard that the workers weren't happy. His phone was ringing with inquiries that turned into new employees.

One of my favorite methods of recruiting comes from author, Catherine Fyock. This method makes use of what are known as "Talent Scout Cards." One retailer, in search of ways to find new people, made up cards, a little bigger than a business card. He and his managers took them wherever they went. When they were out shopping or dining, and they found an employee who was exceptional at giving service, they gave the individual a card. The card had the name of the company with a toll-free number to call. It thanked them for their exceptional service, and stated they were always looking for superior service people. It also stated the opportunities and benefits of working for them (Fyock, 1993).

Using the Net

Thousands of young professionals are obtaining jobs just by surfing the Internet and posting their resumes on it. Since Generation X'ers are so adept at using this technology, the Net becomes a logical and ideal place for you to find good, young workers who are looking for entry level positions, or who want to make changes in their lives.

It's estimated that as many as three million people are using the Internet, either looking for jobs or searching for qualified employees (Dixon, 1995). Many highly technical jobs are being advertised solely on-line. This process may well alter the way people find employment in the future. In fact, a whole new cottage industry has grown out of searching and recruiting on-line. It's a good idea to find out how you can take advantage of this opportunity.

Customers and Vendors

Retailers, restaurants, banks, and hospitals often advertise to their own walk-in customers. This can be done with signs, posters, and flyers. Some stores and restaurants put their flyers next to the cash registers. You never know when customers are unemployed or thinking about a change. Sometimes, your advertising can help them make the shift.

Don't forget about vendors as a resource. Many smart managers frequently ask their vendors if they know anyone who is a quality employee and looking for a new job.

Employee Referrals

Start asking your employees if they know a friend or relative who is looking for employment. Ask them to advertise for you by word of mouth. Employees are a good source for two reasons. First, they won't bring in anyone who is a slackard because it's embarrassing, and it makes them look bad. Second, they don't want to have to take up the slack and work harder because someone they brought in is not doing his or her job.

Reward your people in some manner for bringing in a quality employee. It gives them the incentive to look for more. Some companies reward just for getting a friend or relative in for an interview, even if they aren't hired. Other companies run a contest for the employee who can bring in the most new employees. The contest ends in a grand awards ceremony complete with cash prizes and/or vacations.

Try asking the newly hired employee if they know anyone who is looking for work. It's a good idea to ask them immediately because they won't have any negative attitudes or ideas about a new job or company. They'll be more open to suggestions.

Displaced Workers

This is the group of workers that have lost jobs due to mergers, acquisitions, re-engineering, downsizing, or technology. Looking for these people requires a proactive approach. You need to scan the papers for news about plant closings, company buyouts, or layoffs. Contact their human resources department. This is particularly true in the manufacturing industries. These workers may sometimes need retraining, but often they have the work ethic you want.

Regular Part Timers

There is a segment of the population that does not want to commit to working full time. They may work two or three part-time jobs. They enjoy the flexibility this gives them. They are good workers, and as with the temp agency workers, cost less in benefits. Also, some retired workers want to continue working, but only for a certain amount of hours. You can usually find these people through retirement organizations in your community.

Part Timers Who Want Full Time Work

There is a significant amount of the population who have only been able to find part time work. This is often due to the fact that companies, many times, hire part timers to avoid paying benefits. Some of these workers are looking for full time work after having worked part time in a service industry. Many of them have good interpersonal skills.

In addition, a substantial number of women who have young children work part time. As their children become teenagers, finish high school, or enter college, the mothers then may want full time work. They are mostly in the thirty-five to fifty-five age category, and may need some additional training. On the whole, you'll find that these women have a good work ethic and can handle many tasks at once.

Seasonal Employees

Some businesses will have a greater need for employees during certain times of the year. Find out what groups of workers may be available to work during off times. For example, workers up north in the tourism industry may work during the peak period of May through September, but they may want work during the other months. High school students, college students, and teachers are often looking for work during the summer months. Performers from musical and theater groups may have a period when they are out of work. By the way, this group generally has excellent communication skills.

People with Disabilities

Of all the diverse groups in today's workforce, the one that is the most underutilized is the disabled. There are over 50 million in the United States, but yet their unemployment rate runs as high as 70%. Unfortunately, many people avoid hiring the disabled because they have no idea how to work with them, or fear complications and costs from the Americans With Disabilities Act. These fears are unfounded.

Our surveys of companies that employ the disabled report nothing but praise for them. The disabled employees are hard working, dedicated and loyal, and cost less than other employees, due to their lack of turnover. Companies such as Prudential Insurance, Pizza Hut, and Marriott Corporation have had great success with the disabled.

Prison Release Programs

This is one group that employers are either not aware of, or wish to avoid totally. However, our findings are that prison release programs can be very successful, especially with small businesses where there is physical labor required. These are hard-to-fill positions because nowadays not too many people want to do this type of work. We have interviewed numerous top managers who have found that the prison release workers they hire really want to remake their lives, plus they need another chance. Contact the job counselor at the prison and make them aware of your needs.

Unfortunately, the pool of qualified workers is shrinking. Many of the applicants are minorities, the disadvantaged, the disabled, senior citizens, or people with a history of drug and alcohol abuse. Many who may be qualified don't look and act like the applicants of the past. Today's applicants may not be dressed in a suit, may never make eye contact, and often have interpersonal skills or language barriers that make them very unlike what was formerly envisioned as an ideal candidate.

This is distressing to many people who hire. Candidates don't fit the old molds. The old yardsticks no longer measure what they did before. The old images no longer ring true. *The problem, you see, is not the people, but the "old" concepts.*

As an employer, you need to rethink your idea of what a perfect candidate looks like, or how they behave. Shift your mind set away from the past. Find better ways to get the information you need to make the right hiring decision. In short, create a better system for finding people who will stay on board, and be successful in giving quality service.

Hiring the Right People

You can have great advertising and use all the sources in the world for shaking potential employees out of the trees, but, you have to have the right tools to find the diamonds among the stones. If you make the wrong hiring decisions, all the training in the world won't bail you out. Or, as someone in one of my seminars once said, "if you hire monkeys, and train them, all you have is trained monkeys."

Most people who hire don't have a systematic method to prepare for an interview, nor do they ask the right questions. As a result, they can't make the right choices, and often end up hiring people for all the wrong reasons. Our surveys within companies show that about a half of all new employees last less than five months in the position with which they started. In addition, the average turnover rate in the service companies we surveyed is more than 100% a year.

An effective interview process should be rigorous. This is critical for predicting whether an employee will fit into a customer-driven environment. You should select your people against very high service standards and criteria. You "select in" those that closely match your criteria. You "select-out" those that do not fit. *The people you pick must demonstrate that they share the same customer philosophy and service values as your organization.*

At Country Inns & Suites, they believe that the single most important investment are the people they hire to take care of their guests. In order to be successful in instituting their warm and friendly "Country Culture," they hire "P.I.C.I. people." P.I.C.I. stands for people with passion, intelligence, compassion, and intensity. This serves as the foundation for their Country Culture. As Curtis Nelson, President of Country Hospitality Corporation (which includes both Country Inns & Suites by Carlson and Country Kitchen Restaurants) states, "We are committed to being an organization that truly puts it's people first."

At the Ritz Carlton Hotel Company, a series of four interviews are done. An initial screening takes places before the first of four. Much of the interviewing is behavior based, and many of the questions are about behaviors on past jobs. The Ritz Carlton philosophy is that past behavior predicts future behaviors, and that employees will repeat past successes. It does not matter whether the employee is male or female, young or old, American or foreign-born. They have great success in hiring from a wide diversity of people.

A haphazard hiring approach produces bad results. Some common errors made in searching, interviewing, and hiring include:

- Not having a strategic plan for recruitment
- Not having job descriptions
- Not defining service behaviors and skills
- Treating people poorly when they inquire about openings
- Not reviewing resumes or applications
- Not checking references
- Not understanding the communication patterns of various ethnic groups
- Intimidating the candidate
- Asking the wrong questions
- Talking instead of listening
- Giving away hints on how to answer questions
- Making quick judgments
- Interviewer biases
- Not using assessments
- Overselling the position

By using these methods, you fail to come to a final conclusion about whether the candidate can do the job, and if he or she will perform in a service organization.

Every time you hire someone who is not good at giving service, the entire organization suffers. Bad hires not only create customer ill will, but they affect the people who must work with them and manage them. These employees create stress and disruption in the entire company. Morale is lowered, productivity decreases, and absenteeism increases. Service levels deteriorate more, creating a vicious cycle.

The following are some good and proven techniques that will greatly enhance your chances of picking the right service-oriented people:

Job Descriptions

Start off by reviewing existing job descriptions and job tasks. If you don't have a complete and accurate job description for each employee, now is the time to create them. Job descriptions let employees know exactly what their responsibilities and accountabilities are. They also serve as a basis for establishing more in-depth performance standards. In addition, they provide a foundation for orientation, training, coaching, evaluation, and rewards. More importantly, they let you know what to look for during the interview, and which questions you need to ask. This makes the selection process much more accurate.

One method of creating job descriptions is to ask people in their position to submit a list of about a half dozen major responsibilities they have. Each responsibility needs to be stated separately and to be self-contained. Tell them to begin each sentence with an action verb and write in the present tense. Have your employees prioritize them in importance by numbering them. Compare them and see which ones overlap. These are the main responsibilities.

To this, you can add other duties and responsibilities from your perspective. Also, include the purpose of the position; education, experience, skills, and behaviors required; with whom the person interacts, and any other requirements such as travel requirements or work schedule.

Many people, in creating a job description, omit one of the most important areas. If employees are being hired for service skills positions, they must interface with customers frequently, if not all day. But, in the job descriptions, there is no mention of the service behaviors or skills. *These are critical to the success of your organization!* They must be included in a job description, and serve as a basis for interview questions about service skills and behaviors.

Bob Desatnick, in his book *Managing to Keep the Customer* (Desatnick, 1987), lists the following service behaviors as being critical to service success:

- oral communication skills
- cooperation and teamwork
- problem-solving
- decision making
- sensitivity and concern for others
- dependability
- judgement
- enthusiasm
- high energy level
- flexibility
- adaptability

A job description should accurately reflect the essential job functions. By doing this you will be in compliance with the Americans with Disabilities Act. A job's essential functions are tasks which are basic to that position. You must provide reasonable accommodations to a disabled applicant to enable them to accomplish that job function.

Read the Resumes and Applications

If employers took the time to read the applications and resumes, probably over 75% of all interviews could be eliminated. Resumes give us information the candidate wants us to know. Applications give us information we need to know. Although it may be a boring task, read and compare each resume and application thoroughly. Resumes often stretch the truth about achievements. They are like a beautifully wrapped package, but they don't reveal the contents inside. They are innately designed to hide deficiencies.

Check for lack of information or inconsistencies between the application and the resume. Check for neatness. Neatness counts on many jobs, and a sloppy application shows they don't care. Look for employment gaps or frequent and short-lived jobs. If they show a date containing only the year and not the month, you could have an unexplained employment gap. If they are being deceptive, you don't want them working for you.

Be sure they have signed the application attesting to the fact that the information is correct. It then becomes a document that can be used later for evidence, if the person has not been truthful. Different states have different laws as to the legality of signed applications. Refer to those in your state.

Check References

Many people have found that checking references is a waste of time. Obviously, no one gives a bad reference. The people listed will only give you rave reviews. In addition, personnel or human resource departments are not going to give you any useful information, because they try to avoid lawsuits. Ask your candidate for the name of the manager or owner they worked for directly. Better yet, ask this on the application. Get written authorization from the applicant to call that person. If they decline, you can be sure there is something concerning their job performance or relationship with that person they want to keep secret.

When speaking with their reference let them know that if you don't get the information you need, the candidate can't be considered for the job. From the humanistic standpoint, you may get more information and make the reference less resistant to disclosure. Another approach is to speak with someone in a position above the candidate's former supervisor.

Just listening to the tone and attitude of the reference can give you some hints. If they are quick and guarded, or just state "he/she worked here", you may have cause for concern. If they speak in excited, glowing terms about the candidate, then you know you have a viable candidate. You can learn a lot by listening to what the person says, how they say it, and why they are saying it.

Employee Assessments

If you want to hire people who have initiative, are honest, and are dependable, (three core service behaviors) then you need to find out if they value these behaviors. People's behaviors are driven by their value system. Employee assessments can predict the why of human behavior in addition to the how of human behavior. They can determine whether a person will value, and therefore use, the service behaviors your company values.

Assessments can actually measure a potential candidate's value system. These values, weighed against each, determine how a person will perform in the real work environment. *They determine not only if a someone can perform, but if they will perform.* But, assessments should not be used as the sole determination of whether to hire. Used in conjunction with a well structured interview, they will greatly increase your chances of success. Our consulting firm has helped many companies in hiring sales, service, and management candidates. Interestingly, these same assessments can also be used for coaching and self-development of employees. They help management increase their own effectiveness, as well as their employees.

Some smaller companies may think that testing or assessing employees are just another unnecessary expense. When you weigh the costs of assessments against the costs of hiring, turnover, and unhappy customers, you'll find that the expense is more than justified.

Create a Warm Inquiry System

Many companies, large and small, lose the possibility of grabbing potentially good people due to the way inquiries are handled. Phone calls are not treated warmly. Every time a position is advertised, the person answering the phone gets stressed out by the sheer volume of calls. They may not take the time to convey a warm attitude. People pick up on a negative attitude and shy away from a business, concluding that it isn't a nice place to work.

It's a good idea to sit down with the person who will be answering the phone, and discuss how you want calls to be handled. Be sure they understand how important it is to make people feel glad that they phoned. Explain the importance of courtesy at this critical juncture. Let them know exactly what they are to say, and then role play different scenarios with them. The same fate often happens to walk-in inquiries. The receptionist is often answering the phone, stuffing envelopes, showing people to appointments, and any number of different tasks. Too often, they say very little to the person, and just hand them an application, without a pen, a chair, or a place to write. After people finish the application, they are told, "We'll call you if we're interested."

Prepare the area where applicants walk in to make them feel comfortable. Be sure there are chairs, applications, pens, and writing surfaces. If the receptionist is too busy, assign someone to be the "host" and handle the walk-in inquiries. Again, train them to treat people with dignity and respect and as if they are very important, which they are.

Just as you would use mystery shoppers who act as customers to come in and evaluate your customer service, you can do the same thing with your job inquiry and application process. Have someone pose as a potential applicant for telephone and walk-in inquiries. Have them evaluate the whole process and give you feedback. You could be in for a real awakening.

Pre-Screen by Phone

Use the phone as a method to pre-screen, and eliminate unqualified people. Delegate this responsibility to one of your staff. You want to spend your valuable time interviewing only the best candidates. It's also a money saver when it comes to screening candidates from out of town.

Be sure to ask certain "phone questions" early on that may automatically eliminate applicants. Questions can relate to their availability for overtime or weekend work.

In some cases a car may be required for travel or delivery. Certain positions may require some physical strength like lifting or moving heavy boxes. You want to be sure they can meet the specific requirements of the job.

Ask questions about salary. You want to know how much money they are making now. You also want to know what their salary requirements are.

Ask questions about what they like and dislike about their current job (or past job). This can be very revealing, even over the phone. Include questions about what they are looking for in the job you're offering, and how they would like it to be different from previous ones.

Pre-screening over the telephone not only saves you time, it gives you an idea of what their enthusiasm is like. It gives you clues about their level of interpersonal skills, and how they will sound speaking to your customers. These skills are critical to service success.

Create the Atmosphere

Next, decide where to hold the interview. This plays an important role in the success of the interview and the candidate's decision. Create a warm, favorable climate. The atmosphere must be relaxed and informal. The room should be comfortable, quiet, and free from interruptions. Have your telephone calls held until you are finished.

I recently watched in amazement as a restaurant manager in a major hotel chain was interviewing candidates for a server position. The interviews were taking place at the first table inside the entrance to the restaurant. As the manager attempted to interview, she was also seating people, and ringing up checks on the register. In addition, the interview could be heard by some of the diners seated nearby. Although I had no desire to, by the time I finished dinner, I knew the candidate's complete job history. I couldn't help but wonder how this made the candidate feel!

If you have a receptionist, let them know the candidate's name ahead of time, and have them tell the candidate that you were expecting him or her. All this may seem trivial, but it makes the candidate feel more comfortable.

Seating arrangements are important in creating the right atmosphere. Make sure there are no obstructions or barriers between you and the candidate. Your desk can create a barrier to communication, as well as establish a sense of too much power. Try sitting to the side of your desk at a right angle to the candidate.

Greeting the Candidate

Treat the candidate the same way you would like to be treated in any business situation. You may want to go out to the reception area and personally escort them to your office. Greet the candidate warmly, extend a firm hand-shake, introduce yourself, and name your position. Use their name in the introduction, and also two or three other times during the course of the interview.

Don't barge right into the questions. Use small talk to develop rapport and make them feel comfortable. It's critical that you create a positive impression. It relaxes the candidate and enables them to interview better. This will help to give you an accurate picture of what the candidate is all about. It also creates a positive image for your organization. When candidates aren't treated with dignity and respect, the word spreads quickly. It affects the quality of people who apply for jobs later. *Remember, people who interview are also potential customers!* Their friends and relatives are also potential customers.

A good icebreaker is to offer the candidate coffee or a soft drink. For some reason, coffee seems to be a great relaxant and gets people to open up. One note of caution: don't fill the cup too much. Their hands may be a little shaky, and they may spill it and feel embarrassed.

Develop rapport by talking or asking questions about subjects that are non-threatening, such as the area where they live or the route by which they drove in for the interview. You may find something in common in the application such as both of you may have attended the same school.

Explain the Interview Process

Give the candidate an explanation of the entire interview process. Let them know that you are going to ask the questions for the majority of the interview. Tell them they will have an opportunity to ask questions at the end of it. At this point, you will also discuss the job and your organization in more detail.

However, you need to be sensitive early on to the issues related to disabilities. Explain or give your candidate a job description with the essential job functions (as provided by the A.D.A.). You can't ask the applicant if they are disabled, but you may ask about their ability to perform those duties and tasks related to the job. Explain that you will check references and salary history.

Pre-Write the Questions

Create a written list of good questions. The purpose of these questions is not to find out exactly what they did on previous jobs, but to know how effectively they did it.

There can be a wide gap between being physically and mentally able, and having the willingness to do the job to your standards. After determining that they can do the job, you should find out if they will perform. Will they exhibit the correct service behaviors in your company? Get as much information as you possibly can in order to make the right choice.

In addition, you have to find out if they will fit into your particular store, shop, or organization, under your everyday work situation. You need to determine if their values match the values that you hold critical to achieving service superiority.

Finally, you need to know if they will work well with your staff. Teamwork and internal service in many situations is critical. The attitude of "it's not my job" or "looking out for number one" will simply not fly in today's work environment. Customers demand service, whether they are internal or external customers.

Creating Good Questions

Good questions are simple and precise. The candidate must be very clear about what you want to know. The questions should pose no difficulty for the candidate to answer. Asking very difficult or tricky questions only wastes both of your time, and these produce awkward answers. Your questions should progress in a logical order. You want to be able to get answers that you can delve into deeper. Be careful not to string two or three questions back-to-back. This is confusing. Ask a single question and wait for their response before asking the next one. Concentrate your questions on the areas of education, past job experiences, past on-the-job skills and behaviors.

When I ask participants in my seminars what percentage of time they spend talking during an interview, they invariably state from 40% to 60%. A good rule of thumb is that the candidate should be talking at least 75% of the time, while you're listening. You need to focus and take notes on what they are saying.

Open-Ended vs. Closed Questions

There are many books out there telling candidates how to interview. They list all the common questions and the best answers to get the job. You don't want to ask the same questions everybody else does. Candidates already know how to answer those. You want to ask questions that they aren't expecting, and at the same time, will get them to talk about their past job behaviors.

One way to assure this is by asking pre-planned, open-ended questions. An open-ended question can't be answered with a "yes" or "no" answer. *The old who, what, where, when, why, and how are your best tools.* In addition, you can get people to open up by starting questions with words such as "describe" or "explain." Closed questions, answered with a "yes" or "no," can occasionally be used for clarification or verification. For example: "You mean . . ., Are you saying that you . . ., What you're telling me is that you . . .?"

Stay away from questions that can create legal problems. Questions about gender, age, religion, ethnicity, and arrests should be avoided, unless they are job-related. Some states and local governments have laws that protect areas such as marital status, sexual preference, and the number of children candidates have.

Be aware that you must ask a question about the candidate's eligibility to be employed in the United States. They must provide documents that prove this fact. When in doubt consult with legal counsel on these laws and others related to the Equal Employment Opportunities Act.

The Past Predicts the Future

Base many of your questions around the service behaviors you feel are absolutely critical to success at your company. By having candidates discuss past situations and behaviors on previous jobs, you can better predict what their behaviors will be on the new job. Past behaviors predict future behaviors.

People's basic values, attitudes, and behaviors are established early in life. People tend to repeat these behaviors throughout their lives. For example, look at our spouses or children. We all know how hard it is to get them to change. Modifying their behavior permanently can be considered a miracle!

People find it difficult to make drastic behavior changes. The answers that candidates give you about what they have done before are a pretty good indicator of what they will do in that situation again. As is true with all human behavior, there are exceptions.

If you are hiring a person for a position that has a great amount of interaction with customers, it will require good interpersonal skills, the ability to handle stress, and the ability to deal with difficult customers. You want to ask questions about their behaviors on previous jobs in those kinds of situations.

An initial question could be, "Give me an example of when you had to deal with a really difficult customer." After listening, you can probe further with, "How did it finally turn out?" or, "What did you learn from it?" or, "What would you do differently the next time?" Other questions include, "Tell me more about that?" or "Could you go into more detail?"

Another lead question could be, "How did you handle the stress levels?" Next, you could inquire a little deeper with, "What have you learned about handling high stress levels?" Explore even deeper with questions like "Could you explain what you mean?"

If the job position requires working together closely as a team or giving internal service, you would ask questions related to those behaviors. For example, "Describe a time when you had to work closely with a team on a project." "What did you learn from it about teamwork and cooperation?" Or, "Tell me about a time when you had to go above and beyond in giving good internal service to another department or unit." "How did it turn out?" "What were the results?"

Another good question is the "what if" question. Just create a typical situation or scenario that happens on the job. You ask the candidate what they would do, or how they would handle that situation. Another twist is to give them two alternative solutions to pick from in a situation, and see which one they would choose, and why.

Take Notes

While the person is speaking, take notes. You can't remember everything that is said. Listen intensely, nod, and give verbal and non-verbal feedback. It is up to you to steer the interview in the right direction. Nod your head frequently. Use statements such as "That's interesting, tell me how you did that?" or "Oh really, what did you achieve from that?" These questions show you are really listening, and also allow you to delve a little deeper into their background.

Stay away from too many comments or compliments. Although it may open up the candidate a bit more, it may telegraph the kinds of answers you like. You can nod, or make non-verbal and brief comments such as "Uh-huh" or "I see."

Some companies are video-taping interviews, especially when they are interviewing a lot of candidates. It gives them an opportunity to re-play the interview, and many times, they notice things which were missed or forgotten the first time. Check with your attorney before implementing this for the legalities in your state.

Wrap-up

When finished questioning the candidate, discuss all the aspects of the job and organization that are necessary. If you feel this person is qualified, you may give them a lot more information, and will want to sell the benefits of the job.

Be honest about what you say about the position. A common mistake is to paint an inaccurate picture of what the job is all about. Interviewers sometimes paint a rosy picture of the conditions, overstate chances for advancement, or aren't truthful about why the previous employee left. When a position is hard to fill, don't overpromise. Create a clear picture of what the job is like. Let them know that success in your organization means being successful in handling customers, whether internal or external. Explain the overall benefits of working for your organization. Remember not to oversell.

Encourage candidates to ask questions. The types of questions they ask will give you valuable insight into what they value. It gives you more ammunition in evaluating them. If a person asks questions about salary, advancement, and vacations only, they may be revealing what drives their behavior.

Answer all their questions and be warm and friendly to the end. If you are seriously interested in hiring them, ask them one final question concerning their interest in the position. Use a question such as: "Based on what you have seen so far, how do you feel about this position?" Just like a salesperson, you have to overcome their objections and close the sale. This question will often unearth some fears or misgivings that they may have.

All too often, at this point, the interviewer will tell the candidate the interview is over, and walk them out. But, don't forgot one very important thing. *Explain the next step in the process.* If they are being considered, let them know if there are more interviews, assessments, psychological tests or drug tests to go through. Tell them how and when you will recontact them.

If they are definitely not a candidate, you still want to make them feel good about your company, but don't be overly enthusiastic or give them false hope. In all cases, thank them, and walk them out, maintaining the harmony until the end.

Use a Second Interviewer

In making hiring decisions, the old adage that two heads are better than one holds true. Have a second person interview the candidate with the exact same questions. This throws out the subjectivity and makes the selection more objective. Both people then discuss the candidate together. The two review notes and weigh the pluses against the minuses. This way they can compare "apples to apples." Make your decision based on: can they do what you must have them do, will they perform up to the standards you have set, and do they fit into your organization?

Interviewing Diverse Candidates

A significant challenge exists when interviewing candidates that are from different cultural backgrounds. The interviewer may have their own prejudices, biases, and attitudes. They may prejudge certain ethnic groups or look for qualities similar to themselves. Unless the interviewer is an expert on different cultures, much of what they think or expect is not correct.

In the American culture, we value the outgoing, enthusiastic candidate. Interviewers look for people who smile, make eye contact, and have facial expressions they can read. People are expected to be well rehearsed. They are expected to do their best in selling themselves and their accomplishments. When the candidates are not at all like what the interviewer expects, it often influences the outcome of the interview.

When greeting foreign born candidates, don't expect them to act like American born candidates. Their method of shaking hands may be very quick and limp. Eye contact may be minimal, if at all. They may not show enthusiasm and may not brag about their accomplishments. Be careful not to jump to the wrong conclusions.

You need to find alternate ways to decide whether a candidate is qualified. It becomes more important to check references because the candidate may not express their abilities or skills. Ask the candidate what their previous co-workers would say about their abilities and skills. Give them a typical on-the-job problem to solve, preferably in writing (Thiederman, 1991).

Customer service excellence really starts with the type of people you hire. Don't allow any compromise in this area. You can avoid making concessions if you have a detailed, well-thought out plan. With proper preparation beforehand, and some analysis afterwards, you will greatly increase your success ratio of hiring the right service people for your organization.

Quick Chapter Tips

1. To find good service employees, be proactive and learn to think "outside the box."

2. Some viable places to find good people are recruitment agencies, state agencies, and temporary agencies.

3. Be creative in your advertising and placement of ads. Consider using the Internet, customers and vendors, and employee referrals, as sources for new people.

4. Some sources for workers that are frequently overlooked are: displaced workers, part time workers looking for full time, seasonal employees, the disabled, and prisoners going through release programs.

5. Have a well thought out hiring plan so that you can "select-in" the employees you want and "select-out" those that don't fit.

6. Start by creating job descriptions for each position. Make sure they incorporate the service behaviors and skills needed because they will serve as a basis for interview questions about service abilities.

7. Read resumes and applications. Check for discrepancies and time gaps. Check references as well. Try to speak with someone in a position above the candidate's immediate supervisor. They may be more open in their discussion about the candidate.

8. A warm inquiry system and comfortable atmosphere can go a long way in attracting quality candidates.

9. Pre-screen over the phone. It saves time and gives you valuable clues about the level of a candidate's interpersonal skills and enthusiasm.

10. Create a relaxed, comfortable atmosphere, free of interruptions for the interview.

11. Use small talk to develop rapport, and explain the interview process to the candidate before you start.

12. Create a written list of questions to ask before interviewing. The questions should be simple, precise, and easy to understand. The old who, what, where, why, and how are best. Ask them questions they aren't expecting; ones that will get them talking about past behaviors.

13. Be sure to take notes during the interview. You may want to video tape candidates as well.

14. The selection process will be more objective if you use a second interviewer asking the same questions.

15. Remember, because of cultural differences, foreign born candidates don't interview the same way as Americans. Don't pre-judge them or jump to the wrong conclusions about their abilities because they don't respond in the same manner as natural born Americans.

5

Setting Standards and Measuring Performance: The Infrastructure of Outstanding Service

Dominoes Pizza promises to get the pizza to your door within thirty minutes. The service departments of some auto dealerships advertise an oil change in "thirty minutes or less or it's free." Federal Express guarantees your package or envelope will be there "absolutely, positively overnight." Hyatt Hotels' room service guarantees your meal will be delivered within thirty minutes. Some restaurant chains guarantee your meal in a certain amount of time or it's free, and they actually place a stop clock on your table. Outstanding service companies set very high service standards, and they attain them.

What Are Service Standards?

Service standards are statements that describe service-related tasks or behaviors, and how to perform them. It lets employees know how, and at what point during the customer's service contact to perform high quality service skills. *They are the infrastructure of outstanding service.* To meet these standards, employees need to be trained in all of the expected behaviors required. They need to be tested and evaluated to ensure that they can perform up to the standards set.

Unfortunately, many organizations have set what they think are standards, but these have little effect on raising the customer's perception of his or her overall service experience. We have all experienced the robotic, "Have a nice day" at retail stores or the limp "Bon Appetite" at restaurants. These have become so repetitious that they mean nothing and only turn customers off. Slogans and clichés are not standards. Using redundant statements doesn't improve the level of quality or service. Standards are created by listening to the customers, and understanding their wants, needs, and expectations. It's the customer who determines what ought to happen in a transaction, and how well your organization did what was expected. Standards need to be set at each point of customer contact. This is where perceptions are created in the customer's mind. If that perception is less than what is expected or needed, then you have failed your customer.

Well thought out standards are easily understood by all who perform them. They are attainable by every employee. At the same time, these should not be so exact or inflexible, that employees become dull and boring robots. The standards should be easily observed, measured, and evaluated to ensure they are being reached.

When employees are trained to perform to exact standards, you can constantly reinforce the service message to the customers and the employees. With every transaction, the employee knows he or she is performing in a precise manner to conform to the customer's expectations. It reminds them that the customer is calling the shots. It gives employees a sense of purpose. Your performance standards also become a basis for feedback, evaluation, rewards, recognition, and advancement.

Some businesses make the mistake of creating standards that are too low. They allow for a certain amount of error, and gloat when they beat that set percentage. To those organizations, if they lose a certain percentage of customers and still meet their standard, then they think they are doing great. This, in effect, is telling the customer that if you are one of those who aren't satisfied, it's too bad. You lose!

Can you imagine a company like Federal Express losing just one percent of their packages? How many customers would forgive them? Imagine Delta Airlines crashing one percent of their planes! Would you let a surgeon operate on you if he told you he lost only one percent of his patients on the operating table? Your standards must give the customer nothing less than 100% customer satisfaction! You must set them high.

Determining Service Behaviors

You can't set service standards until you know the behaviors you want from your staff. Begin by compiling a list of the behaviors you feel are absolutely critical for outstanding service. This information comes from staying close to the customer. From complaints, compliments, or surveys, find out what your customers expect, want, and need. In face to face discussions or focus groups, ask customers what are the employee behaviors that make the service outstanding in their minds. The following is a description of service behaviors that your people should have if you want your organization to be considered outstanding in service:

Self-Motivation

People who are self-motivated are self-starters. They frequently take the initiative to begin things with minimal supervision from their manager. They don't need much reinforcement to know they are doing a good job (although they appreciate it). They take the "bull by the horns" and get the job done. They are also very helpful to others.

Enthusiasm

Customers enjoy service people who are excited, cheerful, and upbeat about what they do. These people are energetic and interested in their job, and they show it. They are eager and excited about satisfying all customers. They have a zeal and fervor for what they do, each and every day.

Oral/Written Communications Skills

Good oral communication skills means being able to express information and facts in a clear and concise manner. Employees that effectively communicate with your customers are also able to relate to them in a caring way that makes the customer feel understood. These employees are able to develop rapport and exhibit the "like factor." When customers like your employees, they decide to do business with you again and again.

Written communication skills are the ability to write information and ideas clearly. This includes being able to write a letter to customers in a factual, logical, and progressive manner.

Interpersonal Skills

Interpersonal skills are how employees respond to a customer's problem, and how they consider the needs and feelings of the customer. This category includes an employee's response toward other employees as well, because co-workers are internal customers with distinct needs.

It also includes the ability to show empathy. Showing empathy is the one thing your employees can do to win customers over, particularly when a customer is upset. Empathy is the capacity to feel the frustrations and anger of the moment, and, at the same time, knowing what to do to fulfill the customer's needs.

Listening Skills

A vital element in satisfying customers is the ability to listen. Your people must be able to hear, understand, remember, and act upon the information given to them. They need to focus on the customer's wants and needs. Many times this is difficult because there are a lot of barriers such as noise, which block the process.

Listening is particularly critical when dealing with an upset or irate customer. How employees listen, respond, and act are critical to helping turn a negative situation into one in which the customer is satisfied.

Decision Making

The ability to assess a situation, weigh the facts, and make an accurate and correct decision can often mean the difference between customer satisfaction or an irate customer. This will be discussed in greater detail later in this chapter.

Problem Solving

Problem solving involves the ability to understand the customer's problem and take action to solve it. Often there might be more than one solution. Your customers want solutions that will satisfy their needs; consequently, they have no interest in one that is best for the organization. We discuss problem solving in detail in Chapter Seven.

Cooperation

Cooperation is the act of working together for the mutual benefit of both parties, either customers or co-workers. This behavior is vital to having a positive, friendly, and productive workforce. When internal cooperation doesn't exist, turnover will. It is absolutely essential that you drive home the message of teamwork and cooperation for good internal service. This will be explored further in Chapter Eight.

Reliability

Customers want you to keep your promises. They want you to do what you said, in the manner you said, and within the time frame you said you would.

They want your employees to come through consistently, each and every time. They don't want a roller-coaster ride of sometimes "yes," sometimes "no." Customers tell us in surveys that they don't want employees to run "hot and cold." They want to know that they can rely on your organization, and its people to give them the service they want each and every time.

This category also includes dependability. You must depend on your employees to show up when scheduled and on time. Your people have to be ready for work and willing to utilize their skills and talents to the best of their abilities.

Honesty

Customers are tired of being ripped off. They want to do business only with organizations that are totally above board. They don't want to hear about the fine print or the warranty without teeth. Customers don't want to be oversold, overpromised or manipulated. They want to be warned ahead of time if there can be a potential problem. They don't want to learn that a shipment will arrive much later than expected, nor a product was substituted because you ran out of an item.

Drive this message home to your people: *it is the cheated customer who talks the loudest and the longest.* They will change the story, and will make it worse than it was. Coach employees to be honest and open when dealing with customers.

Flexibility

Customers don't want to be told, "that's not our policy, we can't do that, or absolutely not." *Rigid, narrow-minded rules, whether decided by managers or by employees to make their job easier, only benefit those who created them.* Whenever possible, have employees give customers a choice. Employees need to be empowered to bend the rules in favor of the customer, without fear of retribution.

Handling Stress

Handling one customer transaction after another can make people weary. Working with customers who are demanding, rude, and sometimes obnoxious is stressful! It is emotional labor, and it takes its toll. Be understanding to your front- line staff and show them empathy. Tune into their levels of stress. Send employees to stress management workshops offered at the local community colleges or hospitals. This drives home the message to your staff: You are important, and we care about you.

How to Create Service Standards

After you have defined the service behaviors your organization should strive for the next step is to create the standards of those behaviors that you want employees to exhibit. Again, you can get much of this information from customers, as well as creating the standards with your employees.

In your surveys and focus groups, there are many different questions that can be asked to gather the information, depending on the kind of data you want to collect. Some of the data collected will give you the quantitative information about what your customers want. Examples of this include:

1. Within how many rings should the phone be answered?

2. What is the maximum time allowable to keep people on hold?

3. What is the maximum time allowable before a customer is served?

Not all the data you need will be quantitative. It is equally important, but sometimes more difficult to gather qualitative data. Qualitative data is how the service transaction or experience was handled by the service provider. It answer questions such as:

1. Did the employee greet the customer in a warm, friendly manner?

2. Did the employee handle the experience efficiently and effectively?

3. Did the employee make the customer feel as if they were valued?

4. Did the employee solve the customer's problem?

This is the personal side of customer service, and the part that enables customers to go away feeling really good about the experience.

When gathering information, get input from your employees. They know the behaviors they must have in their daily contact with customers, some of which you may not be aware. An added benefit of doing this is the motivating message you send to your staff: *your opinion is important!* Interestingly, we find that when employees are involved in defining and setting standards, they create tougher standards than their managers do. Consider creating small teams of four to six people to work together on creating service standards.

Begin by naming the behavior with one or two words, such as "teamwork" or "decision making." Next, put the word excellent in front of the behavior you named. Now, write a definition of the behavior. What it would look like if it were excellent? For example:

Decision Making: the ability to gather information, weigh all the facts, and make a sound, accurate decision (on behalf of the customer).

This requires some thought, but the more you work with it, the easier it becomes. Again, ask your employees to help out. Find out what they consider to be excellent cooperation or excellent problem solving.

Be careful! Your standards must be realistic and attainable. You must be absolutely certain your employees are capable of exhibiting the standards of behaviors you want. If you are overly ambitious and set standards of behavior that are impossible to achieve, you risk making employees feel frustrated, stressed, unproductive, and will possibly create turnover.

Next, brainstorm with your employees for examples of that excellent behavior on the job. What does it look like, or what are the results of it? What does an excellent decision maker do? Using decision making (a qualitative standard), they will:

1. Gather all the information necessary to make a good decision.

2. Evaluate the data before making the decision.

3. Consider the implication or impact before action is taken.

4. Make the decision quickly.

5. Implement the decision based on the analysis.

6. Discuss the decision with the proper parties.

7. Evaluate or measure the results of the decision.

For telephone standards you can have a combination of qualitative and quantitative standards. Qualitative examples might include:

1. Answers the phone in a warm, friendly tone.

2. Uses the proper greeting each time.

3. Is patient and courteous with all customers.

4. Thanks all customers for calling.

Quantitative examples might include:

1. Answers the phone within four rings.

2. Puts no one on hold longer than 30 seconds.

3. Transfers customers to the right person, the first time.

4. Returns all phone calls within one hour.

If you have clearly defined the excellent service behaviors, any manager will know what is expected. Any new employee will understand what must be done. They will know what behaviors they are accountable for on the job, each day. Nothing will be left to chance.

Once you have the standards pinpointed and defined, you will be better equipped to hire front-line employees who can implement the excellent service behaviors you want. Now you can look for these behaviors in the interviewing process. You do this by creating questions based on these behaviors. The behaviors will also serve as a basis for measuring and evaluating performance as well as coaching and giving feedback.

Examples of Qualitative Behavior Standards

Enthusiasm—*Eagerly handles customers and is cheerful and friendly in all situations.*

Communication Skills—*Accurately transmits information in a concise manner and is rarely misunderstood.*

Listening Skills—*Able to hear, understand, remember, and act upon the given information.*

Decision Making—*Ability to weigh the facts and make accurate decisions with good outcomes.*

Cooperation—*Always pitches in to help customers, co-workers, or employers, putting the good of others first.*

Reliability—*Can always be depended upon to do what they promise, each and every time.*

Honesty—*Never changes the facts to anyone and is truthful in all words and actions.*

Flexibility—*Ability to give customers more than one choice, as opposed to being rigid or narrow-minded.*

Handling Stress—*Able to handle difficult customers and difficult situations without becoming emotionally involved* (Desatnick, 1988).

Measuring Service Performance

Once you have created standards of service, you need to measure how and if those standards are being implemented. The data from your measurement becomes a guide for making changes in your daily operations. It enables you to solve customer problems and to make changes in the strategies and systems that affect your customers. The total service experience is assessed from the customers' point of view, to determine if their overall perception met or exceeded their expectations. This is a sure fire way to build repeat business.

There are two ways to measure service performance. One is from direct or indirect customer feedback, and the second is from direct or indirect employee feedback. Let's examine both of these:

Customer Feedback

Customer feedback is the best kind of feedback available. This lets you know whether your staff are meeting or exceeding your customers' expectations. Just as you used this information to define and set your standards of behavior, you can also use it to determine if you are achieving your standards.

There are many different ways to collect customer feedback on service performance. Some will give you the same data, but use different methods. That's fine, because it enables you to cross-reference your data to be sure it is valid. The more information, the better. This enables you to provide your employees with accurate and practical feedback. These methods include: face to face interviews, telephone interviews, customer checklists, in depth surveys, focus groups, and mystery shoppers. Let's look at these:

Face To Face Interviews

One-on-one interviews can be a very effective method for gathering customer information. On numerous occasions, people conducting short interviews at retail stores have stopped me and asked questions about the given level of service.

Customers are often in a hurry, and they don't want to take the time to answer. However, when offered an incentive such as a gift or discount, they readily find the time. One real benefit is that customers are often blatantly honest, especially if the level of service is less than expected.

Another good time to collect data is at customer checkout. It takes very little time to ask people if everything was up to their expectations. Some customers are very willing to share their opinion on this point. It is important that you channel that feedback from the point-of-sale to management, in order to make changes.

Make arrangements to go out on site to a customer's place of business. It really impresses customers that you would go to that length to measure your level of service, and get their opinion. Plus, you make it easy and convenient for them.

British Airways has created one ingenious way to gather customer feedback while not actually interviewing customers in person. They have small kiosks or stations at various locations where customers can give their impressions of the service level on videotape. The people are very open and honest because they are talking to a camera, not a person. Each tape is reviewed by British Air, and changes are made based on the feedback.

Telephone Interviews

Phone calls to customers are sometimes thought of as being too intrusive. Our experience has been that customers are often impressed by organizations that call to determine how they are doing. Customers like to do business with those organizations that want to improve their level of service.

You can gather a tremendous amount of information by calling only three random customers per day. Keep the questions short and simple. Make them easy to ask, and easy to answer. Have everyone that calls ask the same questions. Be sure to ask if there is any product or service that you are not providing that they would like to have.

Phone calling key accounts is absolutely critical to keeping them. Too many businesses wait until they have lost the account, and then call to ask why, and try and regain them. This is after the fact. *Be proactive, and keep your finger on the pulse of your customers.*

Customer Checklists

Although you can get great information from interviews, you also need information from a wider customer base. Quick and easy customer checklists provide that base. These are informal surveys designed to get immediate and quick feedback. They are often short, with "yes" or "no" answers, or a scoring from one to five. If the questions are not open-ended, there is an open part left for a comment at the bottom. These can be used after each service transaction to let you know how you are doing on a daily basis.

The number scale can give you a numerical average at the end of a time period (often called a Customer Service Index or C.S.I.). You can set a goal of what you want your daily or weekly score to be. It's easy to check to see if you are reaching it, or how close you are to the goal. Employees want to know how they are doing. You can easily graph or chart the information, and post it for all to see.

A common numerical scale is one developed by Dr. Rensis Likert, from the University of Michigan. The scale is as follows:

1 = Strongly agree

2 = Agree

3 = Neither agree or disagree

4 = Disagree

5 = Strongly disagree

The "yes" or "no" format can be effective. One tire dealership I know uses only three questions about their car service or repair:

1. Was the vehicle finished on time?

2. Was it done correctly?

3. Did the actual cost match the estimate?

At the bottom they have a place for comments. This information is posted daily for all employees to see.

My consulting firm developed a short checklist that can be used for retail outlets, and numerous other organizations.

It is patterned after the main points of our front line training. It is designed to reinforce employee training or may be used to survey customers. These questions also use the "yes" or "no" format:

1. Did we greet you in a warm and friendly manner?

2. Did we make you feel like a valued customer?

3. Did we ask how we could help or offer our assistance?

4. Did we listen to your answers?

5. Did we take immediate action?

6. Did we thank you for your business?

Whatever format or length you decide on, it is effective to change or upgrade the questions, at least yearly, as customers' expectations change over time. You want to be sure that you are keeping up with their changing needs.

In-Depth Surveys

Outstanding service organizations use longer, formal surveys as frequently as monthly. They are carefully designed to gather feedback about the customer's overall experience. In-depth written surveys or questionnaires give you a detailed interpretation of how you are meeting customers' expectations. These are often designed for customers to fill out after the service and mail back. The most important objective is to gather data that will enable your organization to make change.

Surveys enable you to determine whether or not you have satisfied the customer during each customer contact, or at each point of the customer transaction. You can identify the specific areas where customers had problems and take action to correct them in the future. You can ascertain whether or not the customer will do business with you again. You can also learn if customers would recommend you to someone else.

The major hotel chains have been very effective at soliciting data on the customer's overall perception of their stay. Some offer a small gift for filling out the survey before the guest leaves, and this enables them also to gather demographic data.

When creating your questions remember these general guidelines:

1. They should be easy to ask.
2. They should be easy to answer.
3. They should be easy for you to collect and analyze the data.

We have found the best surveys to consist of around twenty to twenty-five questions. Be sure your questions don't have industry jargon or acronyms. After you have finished creating the survey, look for and eliminate any questions that ask the same information. It is very easy to do this without realizing it. Make the questions as "warm and fuzzy" as possible.

Again, consider using a Likert Scale, as it makes it easier for you and the customer. Have a place for comments at the end of the survey. Be sure to include a postage paid reply envelope to make it easy for the customer.

Focus Groups

Surveys and interviews give us answers to the questions we have asked. Focus groups give us information that you need, *but didn't know to ask for it.* These update you on your customers' changing wants and needs. Focus groups also enable you to upgrade your surveys because you learn about customer concerns you had not thought about previously. More important, they let you know how your customers judge you.

A focus group is a gathering of a broad cross section of customers in order to discuss the level of service and the quality of your products. You can use key account or core customers, but don't exclude others as it biases the data.

The group size is often five to twelve people, and the meeting often lasts an hour or ninety minutes. The participants are given an incentive (sometimes cash) for taking part in the discussions.

Although the interviewer has a script with open-ended questions, the interview is often unstructured. The objective is to have the participants talking about their perceptions of doing business with you.

Some questions that are particularly effective are:

1. What's it like doing business with ABC Company?

2. What are we doing that you don't like or you want us to eliminate?

3. What are we doing that you like and want us to continue?

4. What are we not doing that you would like us to start doing?

5. Have you ever had any problem with us as a customer? If so, what was it, and how was it resolved?

You also want to include questions about specific products. Find out what customers like and don't like about them.

Conduct focus groups at least every two months and use many different groups. Look for patterns of complaints or customer problems in the data. Also, look for trends in the good news or positive information. Determine the key reasons why people enjoy doing business with you. These are how your customers perceive you.

There are market research companies that can do the work for you, and many companies use them to save time and effort.

Some organizations have audiotaped or videotaped the responses of focus groups (with permission). Tapings ensure that the information is preserved and can be reviewed. It is more efficient than having an interviewer attempt to capture all the data by taking notes.

The tapes are often played or shown in meetings to every employee. It serves as a powerful learning experience. Employees get to hear, first hand, what the customers' perceptions are, and where they need to improve.

Mystery Shoppers

A mystery shopper is an anonymous person, provided by an outside service, who will come to your place of business, spend time shopping and creating a report that discusses both the positive and negative aspects of the service experience. They can also be used to assess the quality of your telephone service.

Outstanding service companies use these shoppers because they provide trained people who know what to look for. You could bring in a friend or relative to shop your organization. However, they won't be able to evaluate the overall experience as well as a trained and experienced shopper. These shoppers are able to take the entire service experience and break it into smaller components that create the overall perception, and then evaluate it objectively.

When you put this information together with information taken from surveys, interviews, and focus groups, you have a wealth of feedback from which to make changes. However, the data is only as good as the way you use it to make improvements.

Employee Feedback

Your employees face your customers daily. They understand the challenges of satisfying your customers every time. They know what your customers expect. Your staff deals with the problems your customers sometimes face with a new product or service. Employees are a vital source of customer feedback. They have distinct opinions, based on first hand knowledge, of what can be done to improve service. Glen Drasher, Vice President of Marketing for Country Hospitality Corporation states, "It is equally important to research employees, as their insights lead to major breakthroughs. The data collected from employee focus groups and self administered questionnaires really keeps you on track." There are two very effective ways of gathering that information from them:

Employee Service Audit Or Survey

It has been my experience, in surveying many different organizations, that few of them do any kind of employee audit or survey to evaluate customer service. Many companies do employee attitude surveys, or customer opinion surveys, but few actually survey their employees on the one subject of service. You need this information. It verifies or validates the information you gathered from your customer surveys, interviews, and focus groups.

A customer service audit given to employees serves as an assessment tool and a communication tool. It enables you to evaluate the overall views of how employees perceive the quality of service they give. At the same time, it enables people to have a say in their everyday work. This is a very strong need with today's workforce. Employees get a sense of ownership of the suggestions as well as a strong sense of achievement when their suggestions are adopted.

An effective audit can also identify:

1. Productivity problems and their causes

2. Weaknesses in hiring service-oriented people

3. Areas that need training

Basic Audit Guidelines

1. Announce the audit and its purpose two weeks in advance.

2. Announce that the audit is confidential and anonymous.

3. Don't conduct the audit at peak times, holidays, or vacation months.

Concentrate on the core areas that directly affect the level of service. An audit that our consulting firm developed uses questions that can be answered with a "yes" or "no," and has a place for comments at the end of each section (Losyk & Preziosi, 1990).

A "yes" answer indicates that employees feel that the skills, knowledge, or policies are on target. A "no" answer indicates an area for change, improvement, or training. A sample question from each section of the audit are as follows:

1. Policy

   Does your organization have a written customer service policy that has been issued to all employees?

2. Staff

   During the interview process, are applicants asked questions to determine if they have the proper service attitudes and behaviors?

3. Training

   Does every employee receive training about the importance of teamwork to maximize customer service?

4. Service Standards

   Is every employee aware of the service standards established by the organization?

5. Opportunity Analysis

   Does the organization know the exact length of time (or cost) it takes to satisfy a customer complaint?

6. Productivity

   Is service quality maintained as productivity increases?

After tabulating the results by categories and questions, the next step is to study the data for its meaning and implications. More importantly, organize the data in a way that is meaningful to your staff, and present it to senior management to make the changes.

Your people will expect you to implement change based on the audit. If you don't follow through on areas of concern to the majority of employees, don't bother undertaking any audits or surveys in the future because employees will feel it is worthless.

Employee Focus Groups

Employee focus groups are a very effective source for obtaining information on how customer service is delivered, from the employee's point of view. Refer back to the section above on customer focus groups, and follow the general guidelines, except for the audio or videotaping. Concentrate your questions on employees' opinions and recommendations for improving the service levels, and on how to eliminate service barriers that exist in employees' daily routines. Have separate focus groups for supervisors and managers because front line people will not be open or honest if they fear retribution from superiors.

The information must be collected, tabulated, and analyzed. What's more, it has to go to top management for changes to be implemented. Top management should communicate downward the changes to be made as a result of the focus groups. Again, the proof is in the pudding. After you have told them the changes that are to be made, be sure to make them.

Some Guidelines to Consider Once You've Started:

Once You Start, Don't Stop

Once you set standards and begin measuring service performance, don't stop. *Measurement must be forever!* Otherwise, you send out the message that you weren't serious about it. Setting standards and measuring how you are doing is a never ending process.

Measure Often

The superior service companies measure frequently. Their interviews, phone calls, and checklists give them feedback on a daily basis. In-depth surveys and focus groups give them monthly and quarterly feedback. If measurement is infrequent, today's data will be outdated in a short period of time. Remember, customers' expectations and needs change. You must stay tuned to those changes.

Measure Perceptions vs. Expectations

If you have done your homework and listened to your customers, you should know what they expect. Measure the perceptions they went away with and compare it to their expectations. Find out if they were satisfied at each point or "Moment of Truth" during the service experience. If they weren't satisfied, find out why, and take action. If the customer's perception is less than the expectation, it is unlikely they will do business with you again.

Measure Both Qualitative and Quantitative Performance

Knowing how quickly someone answered the phone is just as important as knowing it was done in a happy and enthusiastic manner. Gather both kinds of information. The comments about how someone did something can often reveal the time frame within which they did it.

Log All Negative Feedback In an Accessible, Central Location

One area I have found, where many organizations are weak, is not getting the information out to employees. The data needs to be accessible to all employees. It should show any noted trends or patterns. Every employee must be aware of negative customer comments or feedback that is a direct result of their individual or unit's service. This information should not be used to humiliate or punish. It should be presented in a relevant manner and used as a learning experience. All customer complaints need to be discussed along with the proper manner in which they are to be resolved.

Post Charts and Graphs

Visual displays such as charts and graphs of timely customer feedback have a dramatic impact on employees.

When the results are posted for all to see, they serve as a powerful reminder of the importance of service. These show people the picture of where they are at in relation to where they need to be. The posted results create excitement and high morale when the employees see they have met or exceeded their goals.

Make Changes Based On the Data

Posting the data by itself is not enough. The information needs to be used to solve problems, create new systems and processes, and set new performance goals. Never collect and display data unless it will be used as the basis of some change or improvement.

Setting standards enables your organization to achieve the levels of service your customers expect. Measuring performance supplies the valuable data to discover what changes need to be made in order to succeed, and once the pinnacle of service superiority has been achieved, measuring performance will keep you right there at the top.

Quick Chapter Tips

1. Service standards should be well thought out, easily observed, measured and evaluated. They can't be set so high that they frustrate employees, nor so low that they do nothing to improve service.

2. Know the behaviors your customers expect from your staff before creating the standards.

3. Use surveys and focus groups of customers as well as employees for creating the standards.

4. Once service standards are created, they need to be measured. Measurement is a guide for discovering if customer expectations are being met and provides a basis for making necessary changes.

5. Customer face to face interviews, telephone interviews, checklists, in depth surveys, focus groups, and mystery shoppers along with employee audits or

surveys, and focus groups should be used to measure service performance.

6. Measurement must be forever if customers are going to view your organization as superior in service. It must be done frequently because customers' expectations and needs change. Measuring performance assures that you will remain a leader in providing outstanding service.

Arming Today's Workforce for Service Superiority: The Training Edge

Obtaining consistent and total customer satisfaction doesn't just happen. It's the result of constantly doing the basics the right way, each day. Training is a crucial element in being able to perform those basics. *Training catapults people to go above and beyond for the customer.*

Many companies allow new employees to serve customers with very little, if any, training. This "baptism under fire" is very stressful to the employee and contributes to turnover. It also drives customers away because their expectations can't be met by an ill-prepared staff. Imagine if doctors, pilots, or police officers were allowed to do their jobs without any training!

The training commitment must start from the top. Presidents, C.E.O.'s, and owners all must believe in the value of the training investment. But more than that, they must be seen as "champions of training." This means they should frequently discuss its benefits with top and middle management, and the front line, or actually be involved in the training.

Some C.E.O.'s become part of the actual training process. When British Airways undertook its massive company wide service training program, Sir Colin Marshall, C.E.O., made personal appearances at many of the training seminars. When Scandinavian Airlines implemented its service training, President Jan Carlzon personally conducted part of the top management training. Horst Schultze, President and C.E.O. of the Ritz Carlton Hotel Company, conducts one leadership seminar per year at each hotel. In all of these examples, *the message from the top is simple, yet powerful: training is critical to our success with our customers.*

Total customer satisfaction through proper training has long been a competitive edge for many top companies. The common denominator of these successful companies is that they train, train, train, and quietly reap the rewards. Many of these companies invest up to three percent of annual gross sales on their training.

These "Service Superstars" realize that if service superiority is to be achieved and maintained, learning must be intertwined with work as an ongoing process, not just scattered, unconnected events. Total customer satisfaction cannot be left to chance. *There must be a well defined strategy, and that strategy must have training as an integral part if it is to succeed.*

A recent study conducted by researchers at Harvard University and the University of Pennsylvania with Ernst & Young consulting firm found that companies that train employees, get them involved in the decision making, and implement total quality management practices (T.Q.M), are rewarded on their bottom lines. These companies had significant increases in stock prices, higher market values, and significant productivity gains (Barciela, June 11, 1995).

The companies that have made long-term commitments to customer service training have immediately realized positive results. These include: Ritz Carlton Hotel Company, Disney, Xerox, I.B.M., Texas Instruments, Motorola, Honeywell, and Federal Express. This commitment leads to happier and more satisfied customers, which builds repeat and referral business. It also results in higher employee self-esteem, increased performance, greater productivity, less turnover and decreased costs. In short, training becomes a motivator in the high performance workplace.

These "superstar" companies see service training not as an expense, but as a vital tool for impacting their bottom line profits. You too must look upon it as an investment rather than an expense.

Preliminary Training Considerations

To create any kind of training program, a well thought out plan is necessary. You can't afford to jump "head-first" into a program without thorough preparation. Before you begin planning for training in customer service, think through the following basic considerations.

Who Will You Train?

Is it only your "front line" or direct contact people such as sales staff, counter people, customer service representatives, technicians, and the receptionist? *Service is everybody's business throughout your entire organization.* The same message must be given to all employees at all levels. Developing a service culture throughout your company takes commitment from everyone, so everyone needs training!

Jan Carlzon, President of Scandinavian Airlines (SAS) states, "If you are not serving the customer, your job is to serve someone who is." "Backroom" employees, such as accountants, maintenance staff, and security may not serve your customers directly, but part of their function is to serve other employees or departments internally. They impact everyone else, directly or indirectly. Training these often forgotten people creates better internal service.

If managers and supervisors are to reinforce correct behaviors and skills, they must also go through the basics of what the front line is learning. A crucial mistake I often find is that companies will send their front line staff to training, but their immediate supervisors have no idea what new skills and behaviors the front line has learned. They don't know what to look for, nor which behaviors to reinforce.

What Service Behaviors and Skills Do You Want Employees to Know?

What do you expect your "front line" employees to exhibit and perform after the training? First, identify the service behaviors and skills that are imperative to customer satisfaction in your company (see Chapter Five). But, how do you find that out? *Pay attention to the customer. Ask them what is important.*

Have you written these behaviors in terms of standards? Are these behaviors defined in terms of what is exceptional behavior, as opposed to what is only satisfactory, or unsatisfactory? If you want employees to exhibit exceptional service behaviors, then you must define specific behaviors and train specifically to those standards. Again, those standards must be in terms of what the customer wants and needs.

What Are the Current Needs of Your Employees?

What do they already know, and where are they lacking in knowledge, skills, and experiences? Identify and assess each employee's performance or where his or her service level is failing. You can gather this information by surveying employees on what they feel their specific needs are, and where they feel they need improvement.

Think differently about the training needs of new employees versus veterans. Although the ultimate goal is to have everybody at the same level, the veteran may achieve that proficiency faster or easier.

As Yogi Berra once said, "You can see a lot just by observing." Managers and supervisors need to watch employee behavior to uncover deficiencies and areas needing improvement. Observe how they interact with customers.

Annual performance appraisals are also a good source of information. Customer surveys, feedback, and focus groups are ideal tools for discovering areas where training is vital. From all this information, you can design the curriculum they need.

Determine whether employees have ever been trained in a deficient area before. If they have been, then you need to know why they are not exhibiting that behavior or skill proficiently. It may not be a training problem. There may be a fault in the system or the process by which the work is done. It could be a language or cultural problem. In some cases, it just may be an attitude problem. Whatever the case, find out why the employee is not doing the task or exhibiting the proper behavior, and see how you can help.

Who Will Create and Deliver the Training?

Do you have the time and staff to create your own specific program, or do you need to go to outside resources for available seminars or workshops? Buying a "canned" or generic program or a video taped program will most likely not meet the specific needs or goals of your company. Having management, with internal trainers, or outside training consultants, create a program designed for your unique needs is much more effective. The training has to be targeted to your company and your people. Although the expense is greater, the return on your investment is well worth the money.

How Are You Going to Know
If the Training Worked?

Proper training will create a change in behavior and attitudes, or improve skills and upgrade abilities. What form of measurement will you use to determine whether the behaviors or skills have changed? You need to know which part of the training worked, which didn't, and why. Find out which part of the training should be expanded or omitted. You also need to know what obstacles prevent behavior changes from taking place. Finally, determine what kind of ongoing customer problems still exist.

One simple way to find out is by testing. For some reason, testing after training is not being done enough. Just as you would pre-test before training to determine what is needed, you have to post-test after training to get the results. You must be able to quantitatively measure the difference to know if the training was effective.

Consider establishing a mechanism for auditing quality of service before and after training. Again, customer surveys and focus groups, along with employee surveys or internal audits can help you determine whether training was on target. Create a customer service index that measures customer satisfaction based on the number of complaints and other feedback (see Chapter Five).

Find out how much of your sales is repeat business. Measure the increased use of products and services after the training period. Find some method, specific to your company, that measures your success in reaching your training objectives.

What Kind of Reinforcement System Will Be Used?

Your managers must be trained in how to coach employees, give positive feedback, and correct on-the-job performance deficiencies. They need to spend time with the front line doing on-the-job training. Employees want and need to know how they are doing. Today's young workforce, in particular, needs feedback (see Chapter Three).

After training is over, your people will need their "training wheels" to make the training stick. Employees don't make an immediate transfer of training to their job. It takes two to four weeks for people to make a permanent behavior change. During that time, it is critical that supervisors and managers do whatever they can to encourage the new behaviors. This means creating the right atmosphere and rewarding and recognizing the right new behaviors to ensure repetition (see Chapter Ten).

Consider implementing a Buddy System after training. Have two employees work together as "buddies." This allows them to observe and check each other's progress. This way, they can assist each other. It speeds up the transfer of learning. It's also effective to link a new employee with a veteran, who can act as an "on-the-job" trainer.

Managers need to be able to conduct an effective performance appraisal. This evaluation process should be tied directly to the behaviors for which your employees were trained. Finally, managers have to be trained in dealing with problem employees and know how to terminate those who can't or won't ever meet the service standards for which they were trained.

When Does Training Begin?

An effective strategy for training starts with the employment interview itself. This is where the values and philosophy of service excellence are first explained to the applicant. This discussion should be at the end of the interview, after you've questioned them (see Chapter Four). At this point, potential employees learn that their success in working with your company is based upon their demonstration of your organization's expected standards of service behaviors.

After hiring new candidates, put them through some kind of orientation program. This can be in formal classrooms, or just one-on-one discussions. This is where you explain how and why things are done.

One of the mistakes, I frequently see with orientation programs is that they only give information on policies and procedures. New hires are told about pay, benefits, and hours. Often, employees get a long dissertation about all the things they can't do.

Orientation for new employees has to include training. Some companies put people on probation to see if they work out. During this time they receive no training. Too often, management does not want to spend the money. But, think about the amount of money lost if that new employee runs off customers due to lack of training! More is lost than what would be spent in training. Also, think about the message an employee on probation gets at the beginning. They are being told that they may not be good enough to cut it. *This just may become a self-fulfilling prophecy.*

Orientation programs are the time and place to educate your new employees about responsibilities, accountabilities, performance expectations, standards of behavior, and performance appraisal methods. All this information will again be reinforced in classroom training and on-the-job training and coaching.

First impressions are critical. Those first few hours may determine the kind of service employee a person will be, or how long he or she will stay with your company. See that the new employee gets a warm introduction to and reception from the supervisor and employees with which they will work. Try and do this yourself. They need to feel accepted.

Using the Buddy System with a veteran will make the person feel comfortable by knowing they have one person they can go to, and not feel stupid in doing so. They need someone to give them answers. Have that buddy lunch with them the first week. Be sure you check in with the new employee in the first few days, if even for a short time, to see how they are doing.

Ensure that the new person has a complete job description and understands their responsibilities. Go over the service standards for his or her job or team. Let them know that they have ample time to master new skills and learn new tasks. Don't make them feel they must be perfect immediately. Always eliminate the fear factor.

At the Ritz Carlton Hotel Company, new employees go through two days of orientation at the hotel site, which includes service philosophy, standards, and quality. Top management gets involved, taking part in the orientation. On the twenty-first day, employees go through an additional orientation. Instead of telling employees how to do things, they are asked how they are doing. Management and employees discuss their mutual concerns, and staff members are given suggestions for improving their performance.

At Walt Disney University, the training school for Disney employees, a day and a half of orientation is required. This includes company philosophy, culture, and goals. Employees (who are termed "cast members") then spend an additional day in a division, such as Resorts.

General Service Training Topics

David Kearns, former CEO of Xerox Corporation states, "Training should integrate the strategy of the company, the direction of the company, the vision of the company, and the skills and behaviors that people need in order to get the job done" (Carnevale, 1990, p.11). The following is a guideline for some of the general subject areas that are essential to a successful customer service training program.

Service Mission, Service Vision, Service Values, and Service Philosophy

If your company does not have a specific service mission, vision, or philosophy, then get one! The *first thing* employees need to know is that your organization is totally dedicated to the wants, needs, and expectations of your customers. That commitment must come directly from the owners, or the President and C.E.O. Top management has to create a vision of what the company should look like, and how you are going to get there. This vision needs to be communicated to all.

The Basics

As you saw in the first chapter, today's workforce is very different in terms of their ethnic backgrounds and educational levels. With immigrants continuing to enter the country, many bring not only language barriers, but also a lack of basic skills, as some did not receive a proper education. In the United States, some of today's young people, although computer whizzes, often lack many of the basic skills needed to make them functionally literate. Often, they come out of school without the level of education needed for the workplace.

It's becoming more and more a responsibility of businesses to train people in the basics. This includes English, reading, basic math, and written and oral communications. If your entire company is to be responsible for giving great service, then employees must be trained in the basic areas that enable them to function on the job. With these basic skills in hand, your staff can concentrate on more important things, like service.

Company Products and Services

This is an obvious one, but again train everyone, including receptionists and "backroom" employees, in the essentials of products or services. Don't leave it to chance. An employee who normally doesn't have customer contact may have to answer a question about a specific product or service. Customers don't want to hear, "that's not my department," or "I am only the receptionist." When customers get their questions answered immediately, it greatly enhances the professional image of the service provided by your company.

Job-Related Skills

Your employees must be trained thoroughly in the use of available office tools and technology for their everyday job. This includes proper usage of phone systems, computers, copiers, and fax machines, and anything else that helps them to do their job. Not only does this increase productivity, decrease mistakes, and lessen stress, but it upgrades the perception of staff professionalism to your customers.

Behaviors and Attitudes

You must decide what job behaviors are necessary for service success. You have to intensely know your customers, and what satisfies them. Then you train and teach those behaviors to your employees and reinforce what was learned.

The subject of attitudes needs to be addressed in training. Admittedly, it's hard to change attitudes. It's impossible to know what went into twenty or thirty years of creating the attitudes and value system of an individual.

Don't waste your time playing psychologist. Instead, instruct people on how their attitudes affect the decision of customers in buying your products or services. Employees need to be aware of how their attitude is projected, and how it also affects co-workers. It reveals itself in their appearance, voice, gestures, facial expressions, and eye contact. Let them know that their attitude may be the only reason customers do business with you, and not the company down the street.

Problem Solving Skills

A frequent complaint I find in our customer surveys is that employees often can't solve customers' problems. Many times, they don't have enough information to make a solid decision or aren't creative enough in their thinking to find a solution. The ability to be innovative and solve your customers' problems drives customer perceptions of service through the roof! Solving customer problems, however, cannot be left to chance. With proper training problem solving abilities can be greatly enhanced.

Many companies have begun to bring stark reality into the classroom. They invite some of their customers to be part of the problem solving sessions. Customers give insight into the actual problems they are having, and how management and staff can go about solving them. It's a real eye-opener.

Suggested Front Line Training Subject Checklist

Professional Image

_____ Appearance

_____ Courtesy

_____ Depth of knowledge

_____ Confidence

_____ Flexibility

_____ Sense of humor

Interpersonal Skills

_____ Greeting and smile

_____ Handshake

_____ Eye contact

_____ Vocal quality

_____ Teamwork and teamplay

Relationship Building

_____ Developing rapport

_____ Empathy

_____ Care and concern

_____ Making customers feel important

_____ Proper questioning to determine needs

_____ Product and service knowledge

_____ Problem solving

_____ Creative thinking

_____ Handling exceptions

Communication Skills

_____ Understand the two-way communication process

_____ Recognize barriers

_____ Understand body language

_____ Improve listening skills

_____ Understand the importance of perception

_____ Know negative impact of bias and prejudice

_____ Handling upset or angry customers

_____ Managing personal stress

Telephone Techniques

_____ Proper answering

_____ Putting people on hold

_____ Proper transferring

_____ Taking messages

_____ Statements to avoid

_____ Making callbacks

Process Improvement

_____ Total Quality Management

_____ Process improvement tools

How Often to Train

Every employee needs service training twice a year, whether they just started or are veterans. The topics listed can be covered in one or two day's training. The number of seminars your staff needs depends upon their training needs, the number of people to be trained, and your budget allocations.

Within six months after initial training, half day training seminars are essential for follow-up. Concentrate on behaviors, attitudes, and solving customer problems at that time. New problems will arise as new products and services are introduced. Of course, technical training must be updated whenever the technology is changed or improved.

A good example is Ritz Carlton's commitment to on-site training. It can be seen throughout their organizational structure. In addition to a hotel quality leader and repeat guest coordinator, each department has a training manager. Every employee must obtain certification in their position. The training manager signs off on each employee's certification after testing and observation.

At Walt Disney World, each division does its own training. Initial on-the-job training can last up to a month. After that, training is ongoing, with retraining, job enlargement, and job enrichment provided as needed.

Encourage your people to attend seminars off site for further development. This can be a great motivator for people. There are many companies that provide excellent public seminars at local hotels for a fair price.

If you don't have a company or departmental newsletter, then consider starting one. This is another method for continually training and reinforcing the service message.

Let it be filled with service refreshers and reminders. Let it sing the praises and recognition of people doing an exceptional job. Let people know who went the extra mile or saved the company from losing an account or a customer. Constantly send out the message that service is critical to success. This all adds to creating a service culture.

Management Training

To ensure a high level of quality and customer satisfaction, it is imperative that management be thoroughly trained. Managers and supervisors must be able to lead and motivate their people. They can't achieve results, and be held accountable for those results, without being trained themselves.

Top management needs to be trained in how to create a vision and then a blueprint for making that vision a reality. Middle management has to learn the quality improvement process, and all the tools that it entails.

Walt Disney World has its own Management Development Program consisting of a series of modules that new managers must complete on their own. As they work through the modules, managers answer questions and have a series of tasks to complete. They have a specific time frame in which to complete those modules.

The management teams at all Ritz Carlton Hotels take seminars on basic management and leadership skills. Additionally, all are required to take one, four-hour seminar per month and become certified in the hiring process and leadership skills.

Suggested Management Training Topics

- Strategic planning to implement a service vision
- Service behaviors and attitudes
- Management's role in customer satisfaction
- Leadership skills
- Hiring service oriented people

- Oral/written communication skills
- Coaching and feedback skills
- Reward and recognition skills
- Managing internal service
- Team building skills
- Handling employee conflicts
- Handling employee discipline
- Problem solving skills
- Quality improvement process
- Conducting performance evaluations
- Terminating non-performing people
- Stress management

What Kind of Training Format Works Best?

From doing over 1,000 customized seminars, I have good insight into the methodology that works and what doesn't work. We know that adults learn best in an atmosphere that is relaxed and fun. With the effects of TV, and its graphic images, camera angles, and trick shots, we know people today can get bored very easily. The Generation X'ers, sometimes also referred to as the "MTV Generation," especially, want to be entertained. So training must be stimulating, as well as challenging and rewarding.

The training must be relevant to the trainees in their everyday work. There must be something in it for them. People want a direct benefit that will help them immediately. We have to create real-world scenarios that actually happen in their everyday work.

The training has to be exciting, and frequently "change gears." *The old lecture method just doesn't cut it anymore!* You have to get people involved and participating. They need to be able to process the information and see how it applies. Videos, slides, and overheads have to be used to make points and reinforce the message.

In my own seminars, I use a lot of humor, anecdotes, real-life stories, and fun activities to make my points. People remember the stories, with their vivid imagery, inspiration, or humorous endings. As a result, they remember the point. Adults learn best when they are actively involved, and having fun.

Each person participates or gets involved one way or another. Everyone gets a chance to be a group leader during brainstorming and problem solving sessions. They also do self assessments where they are able to determine their current styles and behaviors in relation to where they want to be. They love the personal insight this gives them. I couple this with real, practical, take home materials that reinforce the learning experience long after the seminar is over.

Group activities, brainstorms, role plays, case studies, use of videotapes, and solving real problems all keep the day fast-paced and moving. I also have people keep a list of things they must go back and do. They create action plans and make commitments to implement the needed changes. Trainees exchange and discuss those ideas in order to have reflection and closure.

We give out prizes at the end of the day for the best ideas. The best compliment is when they say the day went by very fast, or they could have stayed even longer.

Training Immigrant Workers

There are some basic differences to keep in mind in training immigrant workers besides the language barrier. Cultural factors can act as barriers to training and need to be considered if you want the training to work.

To some foreign born people the training experience can be threatening. They may fear being humiliated, or that they will lose their self-esteem in the process. If they are embarrassed in front of a group, it will prevent them from valuing the training experience. This will cause resentment and passive resistance on their part. Eventually, they will just give up. Enable people from diverse cultures to feel as comfortable as possible during training. Create a positive atmosphere that allows them to feel good about themselves. Let them know that you respect their culture, and in no way demean it or lessen its existence.

It's best to start in small progressive steps. Don't inundate them with too much information. It's difficult for some immigrants to translate a lot of material at one time, and it's more difficult to retain translated information.

Pick your words carefully, and say them slowly, with pauses. Use words you are confident they will understand. Repetition and review are important if they are to retain the information. Your words may not translate the first time. Be careful not to use acronyms or industry terms they may not understand. Above all, don't talk down to them in any manner. Use lots of one-on-one positive reinforcement. Remember that many foreign cultures are embarrassed by public praise and recognition.

Use simple visual aids and don't confuse them. Easy to understand overheads, drawings, and diagrams will work wonders. Have each visual aid communicate one topic or idea. Physically demonstrate a task whenever possible.

If you are training employees yourself, or are communicating with immigrants in a meeting, and no one is asking questions, don't assume that you are completely understood. For some immigrants, it's embarrassing to admit they don't understand. They may also feel they are insulting the instructor because questions may imply that the instructor hasn't been thorough in the explanation.

People with heavy accents sometimes are very quiet during training. They are reluctant to initiate a task, and they may refrain from being involved in an activity because they feel self conscious about their accent and ability to communicate.

I experienced this problem when I was doing training for a major hotel chain. On this particular day I was training the restaurant bus staff, who were all from Central and South America. Most of them understood me completely and were enthusiastic about the training. One young man in the class was very animated and enthusiastic in his body language. He was nodding and smiling throughout my session. During one of the breaks, I walked over to him and told him that I noticed he seemed to be enjoying the seminar, and I then asked if he had any questions. He looked down in embarrassment and said, "No speak English." I learned not to assume by someone's body language that I'm communicating. Some people from foreign cultures often want to please their boss or instructor, or they may just fear losing their job if they don't understand.

Your expectations for their success in training should be high. If you expect slim results, you will get just that. Let them know, within time, you expect them to perform just like everyone else. Inspire them to achieve that goal.

Cost vs. Benefit

You may be concerned at this point about training costs. How much money should be allocated for effective training programs? This figure will vary from organization to organization depending upon your response to the basic considerations discussed earlier.

In the U.S., the average company spends 1.4% of payroll on training. However, companies such as IBM, General Electric, Xerox, Motorola, Texas Instruments, and Honeywell spend anywhere from three to six percent of payroll (Carnevale, 1990). Motorola estimates the return of its training investment to be thirty dollars for every dollar spent (Reuters News Service, 1995).

One study done by Citicorp of seventeen superior service companies, found all were very committed to training. They invested as much as one or two percent of gross sales in "formal ongoing training programs" (Desatnick, 1987).

Take your payroll and multiply it by two percent. Multiply your gross sales by one percent. Pick a point halfway between the two figures. This will give you a ball park figure of what you should begin to commit to total training.

At first glance top management, especially in small companies, may view this as a tremendous expense. However, it must be looked at as an investment in human capital, not just a cost without a return. Research has shown that after one year, people trained in the workplace have significantly higher rates of productivity than those that did not undergo training. This rate can be as high as 30% (Bishop, 1989).

The overall costs of training include:

- The cost of the instructor or consultant
- Food and beverage
- Training materials
- Audio-visual equipment
- Use of space (whether on or off site)
- The salary of those being trained during that time frame. Also consider the training time when you are short staffed or must find someone to replace those being trained.

Training is expensive, but if you are going to do it, it pays to do it right. You must create the conditions where people will go back and use the new knowledge and skills. *Your managers and supervisors must be behind training 110%.* They are the ones that can ensure the training investment will be successful. In addition to being role models of the right attitudes and behaviors, they need to reinforce and coach the behaviors within the front line. They must recognize and reward people for changing and improving behaviors. This training investment leads to:

- Higher employee self esteem
- Increased job satisfaction
- Improved morale
- Less absenteeism
- Better quality
- Higher productivity
- Greater company loyalty

In turn, this same investment will lead to increased sales, repeat business, higher customer satisfaction, and will guarantee a profitable niche in your marketplace tomorrow.

Quick Chapter Tips

1. Top management must be champions of training and show their commitment to it in order for training to be successful.

2. Implement a training program by first determining who in your organization needs training and then determine what areas to train in.

3. Decide how you are going to create the training, and the best way to deliver it.

4. Create a system to measure the effectiveness of the training and to find out if changes have occurred.

5. Develop a system to reinforce the training experience. Consider implementing a "Buddy" System.

6. An orientation program, either formal classroom training, or one-on-one discussions is vital to a new employee's success. This is where employees learn about expectations, responsibilities, and expected service standards.

7. General service training should include: service mission and philosophy, basic math and English skills, company products and services, job related skills and behaviors, and problem solving skills.

8. All employees need a minimum of two days of training per year.

9. Management training is critical to achieving service success. Minimum topics should include: interviewing skills, leadership, coaching, motivation, teambuilding, and how to terminate employees.

10. Training should be highly interactive, entertaining, and meaningful to employees. Get them involved in group activities.

11. Be sensitive to cultural differences when training immigrant workers. Some may see training as threatening or humiliating.

12. Look upon training as an investment, not just a cost. Base your training budget on a percentage of payroll and gross sales.

Empowering People to "Power Up" Service

Some people seem to think empowerment is another one of those management fads or the "trend du jour." Nothing could be further from the truth. In fact, if you look at those service organizations that are the leaders in quality and customer satisfaction, you'll see that empowerment is one of the key elements common to their success.

What Is Empowerment?

Empowerment basically allows people to not only make suggestions, but to take action on their own. Their actions aren't restricted by the usual rules and regulations of the company. Employees are highly trained and informed, and are able to make intelligent decisions based on their training, as they confront a new or unique situation. They are provided with the tools and resources to back their decisions.

Peter Block says "While empowerment is a state of mind, it is also the result of position, policies, and practices" (Block, 1987). Systems that create senseless policies and procedures that prevent performance are removed. Employees are taught to "bat outside the box." They are able to make competent and creative conclusions based on the situation and their preparedness. Their ultimate goal is 100% customer satisfaction.

You don't give away your power with empowered employees. Empowerment isn't some perverse form of anarchy. Instead, you're sharing power so that your front line people can make on the spot, common sense decisions. *Empowerment never occurs at the expense of quality, structure, or standards of behavior.*

Empowerment creates a positive, open atmosphere where customer-based decisions can be made. It fosters a climate where quality and service can thrive as people are more in control of their destiny.

It's done by sharing information, knowledge, performance rewards, and the glory and success of the company. All of this enables your people to be responsible and take action for the good of the customer.

Warren Bennis and Bert Nanus, authors of many leadership books, see empowerment as one of management's critical leadership responsibilities. They state: "Empowerment is the ability to generate enthusiasm and vision, and communicate this to people; it is critical in any leadership role" (Bennis & Nanus, 1985, p. 80).

Empowering leaders are open to the ideas of all their people. They listen and act on those ideas. A good example is Sam Walton, the late founder of Wal-Mart. He used to say that, "my best ideas come from clerks and stock people."

These leaders challenge their people to think for themselves. They enable their employees to act on customer issues as they occur. Finally, they act as a coach and mentor, giving feedback and encouragement and allowing their people to excel. Darryl Hartley-Leonard, President of Hyatt Hotels Corporation has said that, "Empowerment is the recognition that employees are not as dumb as employers thought they were" (Nelson, 1994, p. 116).

Let's face it. You as a manager or owner can't be everywhere all the time, and you can't do it all yourself. You must rely on your people. They have to make logical service decisions when you aren't available. They can't tell customers "Wait, while I go find the boss." In fact, customers tell us in surveys that they want people to make decisions, without having to go to a higher authority or through a long, involved process. They want to do business with people who are confident, assertive, and decisive.

Don't be afraid that your people will give away everything but the "kitchen sink." What's the worst that could happen? *Your customer will go away feeling they received outstanding service.* That's far better than having angry customers. Satisfied customers build repeat and referral business. That kind of business costs nothing, while dissatisfied customers costs you dearly.

Technology has helped in the development of the empowerment movement. More and more, machinery, equipment, and computers are controlled strictly by the people who use them. Those workers must be empowered to make decisions in the use of that technology on the customer's behalf.

For example, you've seen the Ford commercial where the front line worker is empowered to push a button that stops the entire automated assembly line. This is done when they see a defect or problem that may create a lack of quality. That front line worker alone makes the decision. They are the manager of the moment. They don't have to ask anyone else. Obviously, this type of empowerment at Ford Motor Company has lead to greater employee pride and satisfaction. Plus, Ford's vehicles have had higher quality in the last few years.

At Disney World, the initial employees that come in contact with the customer, whether it be in person, or on the phone, are empowered to solve customer problems. The customer doesn't get directions to go somewhere else for a decision. There is no wait for an answer. Disney believes that customer service starts and ends with the first employee the customer encounters. Can you imagine what this does for the self-esteem of the employee, not to mention the perception of that customer?

When employees have the power and authority to make decisions, they become more responsible. They look for solutions to problems and feel more committed. More than that, work becomes more meaningful, and they begin to show a sense of ownership. As they are able to exercise judgment, employees gain a sense of achievement. A mindset and culture is born that is creative and innovative.

Remember, it is this innovation that drives customer perception through the roof.

How do you develop empowered people? If you have an atmosphere where people are used to being directed and controlled, it takes some time to make the change. Here are some strategies:

Remove Fear

W. Edwards Deming, a leader in the total quality improvement movement, states in his fourteen points for management: "drive out fear, so that everyone may work effectively for the company" (Deming, 1986, p. 23 & 59).

In order to begin having empowered employees, you need to remove all fears, particularly the fear of making mistakes. If your people fear being fired, they will never use their authority to make decisions on the spot. If you come down hard on your people for making mistakes, you will destroy any chance for them to feel empowered. People will go back to waiting around to be told what to do, instead of doing what must be done.

Does that mean that employees can do whatever they want, and never have to worry about a mistake? Absolutely not! *Never tolerate anything lower than the high service and quality standards that you have set.* Mediocrity, carelessness, and buck passing have no place in your organization. It cannot and must not be tolerated.

However, if bad judgment is made regarding a customer interaction, you can discuss the situation with the employee. This should be used as a learning experience. The employee discovers a better way to handle that situation the next time around. The employee may be disappointed that they made a mistake. But, if you have fostered high self-esteem in your employees, they bounce back quickly. You always want to commend and encourage the attitude that fosters problem solving on behalf of the customer.

Let me give you an example. In one of my seminars, I was discussing what it takes to go above and beyond to satisfy the customer.

I told a commonly known story about Nordstrom's Department Stores. In brief, it is about a lady who wanted to return her tires to a Nordstrom store because she did not like the way the tires were wearing. Nordstrom's took back the tires, and gave her a refund. The group listened skeptically because there was a slight catch. Nordstrom's doesn't sell tires! However, the store felt they would gain a new customer for life by doing this. The mileage out of this story alone has given them many new customers.

Immediately after telling this story, a young manager in my audience raised her hand to tell me a personal experience she had. She had always shopped at stores that offered specially made shoes. She was born with her feet being two sizes apart. She was at a mall, and decided to stop in a Nordstrom's store, where she found a particular pair of shoes she loved.

She told the clerk, known as an associate, about her dilemma. She asked if they would be willing to break a pair. He replied, "No one ever asked me that before, but sure we can." She got the two different size shoes she wanted. Nordstrom's gained a new customer for life. Now, she only buys her shoes from Nordstrom's. Nordstrom's had two other shoes left from a pair that they would never sell, unless they find someone with the exact same size feet, who wanted that style and color of shoes.

It was that employee's lack of fear that empowered him to make a decision. He knew he could solve a customer's problem, and never have to worry about being reprimanded for wasting shoes or money.

But, look at the benefit that Nordstrom's has gained. The young manager has told the story to many people. I've told the story to thousands in my audiences. Thousands more will read about it in this book.

Interestingly, Nordstrom's advertising budget is about 1.5% of sales. In retailing, most chains spend five percent or more. Why the considerable difference? Word-of-mouth advertising is the best kind you can get because it builds repeat and referral business. Best of all, it's free.

Remove the Barriers

Remember when you were a teenager, and it seemed every adult in the world was telling you how to run your life? Your parents, relatives, teachers, and even neighbors all had a hand in letting you know just how far you could go. There were so many rules and barriers preventing you from doing what you wanted that you felt as if you were suffocating. It made many of you rebellious.

Your employees feel the same way, especially with today's "do whatever you want, and do it now" mentality. Many of the younger employees have been brought up with a tremendous amount of freedom. Plus, their hours spent alone watching TV, and working with computers have made them naturally creative.

Many companies put in senseless and needless policies in order to control employees. The mindset is that employees will not perform unless constantly supervised. Workers have no initiative and motivation. People will rebel against this philosophy. But, when you create an atmosphere that supports empowerment, *your people will thrive!* Don't stand over people, and watch their every move. Show your people you trust them. Stop controlling, and start empowering. Just like a parent, you need to learn to let go.

Ask all your people what barriers stand in their way from making decisions or solving problems. Ask them what policies or procedures prevent them from being productive or innovative. Find out what processes are designed wrong, and keep them from giving excellent service. Ask them what they need to create better quality.

You need to keep questioning until you're satisfied that all the barriers that get in the way of top-notch performance are eliminated. You have to listen intently to those answers and implement action accordingly.

Customers see too many non-sensical rules and procedures that get in the way of having the service they want. Unfortunately, many of these policies also make your employees feel incompetent, and hurt their self-image.

For example, you've probably had the experience of writing a check or returning an item at a retail shop. Many stores have a policy where the clerk must call over a supervisor. They do this by phone or intercom, and there is always the requisite five minute wait until the supervisor finally appears. The supervisor picks up the check or return slip, and without ever looking at it, initials it, and gives it back immediately to the clerk. The clerk then finishes the transaction with a long line of customers waiting impatiently.

I have asked many clerks what the purpose of the initials are as the supervisor never looks at what they are initialing. I get answers such as: "I don't know. It's just a stupid policy. It makes them feel important." The front line people have no idea why it's being done, and it certainly doesn't make them feel respected. Nor does it make the customer happy, nor endear them to the store.

I've asked supervisors why this is done. I could never get a logical answer. Instead I hear: "It's our policy. My boss makes me do it. It keeps people honest." So, we have a procedure being practiced again and again, throughout retail America, and the people involved in carrying out the procedure don't know why!

You may have heard the story about the little girl who was watching her mom cook a turkey for Thanksgiving. She noticed that mom was cutting the tail off the turkey. She asked mom why she was doing that. Mom replied, "Why, I don't know. I've always watched my mom do it. Why don't you ask Grandma?" Grandma lived downstairs.

The little girl went downstairs and asked Grandma the same question, "Why do you always cut the tail off the turkey?" Grandma replied, "Why, I don't know. I've always watched my mom do it. Why don't you go ask Great Grandma?" She lived next door.

The little girl, determined to get a logical answer, ran next door. She said to Great Grandma, "Why do you always cut the tail off the turkey?" Great Grandma replied, "Why, honey, when I was young and first married, we didn't have a lot of money. I only had small pots and pans. We couldn't afford to buy a big pot. So, I cut the tail off the turkey so it would fit."

Many retail stores are doing the same thing. It's the same way with many companies who have senseless and almost mind-boggling ways of doing things. Get rid of those procedures. Ask your people a simple question, which takes guts: *"What policy, procedures, or rules do we have in place that prevents you from doing your job or serving the customer?"*

Collect the answers, and sit down and analyze the information. Eliminate whatever is not needed and change the things that can be improved upon. Remember, it is your front line employees who are closest to the customer transaction. They see, hear, and sense things that management does not.

Creativity coupled with the freedom to make intelligent decisions are two of the best ingredients you can use to create an empowered employee. Throw in a large dose of training and communication, and a liberal amount of delegation, and sprinkle in caring and respect. Then, extract the fear, and you have got a very healthy recipe for empowerment.

Hire Diverse People, and Those Who Think Outside the Box

If you want to solve customers' problems on the spot, then you need to find people who can think creatively and come up with unique solutions. That means not hiring people who are strictly "yes people." Hire people who are going to question you once in awhile and who will tell you when there is a better way. Find people who take risks, and don't always go along with the rules. Find people, because of their creative genius, who don't seem to fit in elsewhere. Different personalities can only strengthen your company's ability to solve customer problems.

With today's diverse workforce, you have an opportunity to get a wide perspective of viewpoints. Diversity brings with it a richness of backgrounds. People from diverse backgrounds think differently. They give you a wealth of perspectives, ones you would never get if you had a work-force consisting of only one race or one nationality.

Many studies and experiments have been done over the years on problem solving and decision making with homogeneous versus heterogeneous groups. When the solutions to problems are compared, the heterogeneous or culturally diverse group always finds a more creative solution. Different thought processes create better solutions to customer problems.

Training and Empowerment Go Hand in Hand

Empowerment goes hand in hand with education. Without proper training, empowerment cannot and will not happen. Give your people general guidelines on what they can and can't do for the customer. Inform them that they are expected to use their authority. The more your people know, the more it boosts their confidence. It raises their self-esteem. They are more apt to solve problems and make decisions. They know that they have the power to make positive changes.

By having well-trained employees who can accept responsibility and make intelligent decisions, you don't have to worry about watching everyone all the time. They can take action while you take care of other more pressing issues. Let's look at the type of training that creates empowered employees.

There are many front line people in today's diverse workforce that lack the basic educational skills. Some need assistance in basic math, writing, reading, and language skills. Some of today's young people lack the interpersonal skills needed to deal with people. Although personalities can't be altered, people can be trained to show warmth, friendliness, and courtesy.

Another area requiring training is in your company's service philosophy and values. Your front line people may come from a background with a very different value system. Employees need to know the value system that top management lives by, and how that fits into their everyday work life.

In order to be empowered, your people must also be trained in three other areas: job-related skills, standards of service behaviors and problem solving skills. Unless you communicate your standards, you cannot measure them, and hold people responsible and accountable. Remember that employees don't automatically know how to take care of customers. Young people are not used to serving others. People from different foreign cultures may have different ideas than you about what service is all about.

Any cross-training that is done really helps in being able to make better customer-oriented decisions. This cross training exposure fosters cooperation between team members and departments. It vastly improves communication and internal service.

Some people don't take to empowerment because they feel they aren't trained enough to make decisions. You have to give them the competencies that will enable them to use their power.

The ultimate goal of training is for your people to make common sense decisions about challenges that have not come up before, or are not listed in your standards of behavior or policies book. Training will enable them to make those decisions with confidence.

Let me share with you two personal experiences where the lack of training created a lack of empowered decision making and created near-hatred by customers for the service providers.

Last year I attended the annual convention of the National Speakers Association, at the Washington Hilton in Washington D.C. This is a very exciting meeting, that brings together hundreds of the world's best professional speakers and trainers. At the end of the convention everyone is highly motivated and beaming with enthusiasm.

After about a dozen speakers boarded the bus to return to the Washington National Airport, we noticed a blind lady approaching the bus with a seeing eye dog. The bus driver jumped out of his seat and told her that she could not board with the dog. She stated she was legally blind, and provided the papers to prove it.

We all told him that he had to allow her on board. He said he had to call his supervisor before he could allow her on board. He left the bus and went over to the hotel bellhop stand to make the call.

Unfortunately, the driver's supervisor couldn't be reached. Time started to pass. This very angry group started to yell to the driver that we would miss our flights. He stayed on the phone until he got an approval from the powers that be. He then drove to the airport in an angry and reckless manner trying to make up for lost time.

If the bus driver had been trained properly, he would have been able to make an immediate decision to let her on, and we would have been on our way. People, by law, have been allowed to use seeing eye dogs on public transportation for many years.

The poor lady with the dog felt terrible and kept apologizing to us for the delay. We told her it wasn't her fault, but it was the fault of the driver's ignorance. We barely got to our terminals in time to catch our planes. The driver probably lost about $25.00 in tips. A group of professional speakers now have a great example to tell hundreds of audiences across the country. The reputation of the bus company will be soiled forever, due to a lack of empowerment and training.

In another incident, I traveled to Denver to speak to a group of managers. This was a week after the new Denver International Airport had just opened. I was excited about seeing this state-of-the-art airport. When I arrive at airports, my routine is generally the same. I look for the shuttle services (I stay away from cabs because of the attitudes and horrible driving habits of the cabbies I've encountered in the past).

I found a shuttle van and was told we would leave in a few minutes, as soon as the van filled up. The last passengers to get on were a young lady and her little girl. As we departed, the driver asked for everyone's ticket. He was already curt and had an attitude. The young lady stated she wasn't given a ticket, but was hurriedly escorted to the shuttle so she wouldn't miss it. At this point, he began telling her she had to be given a ticket, or she just didn't bother to pay. They started to argue. He decided to drive around the entire huge airport in a circle, and then returned to where we began. He told her to go to the shuttle counter to "either pay or get a ticket. Otherwise," he told her, "I'll have to pay the company."

Although this company has been in business for many years, there was obviously no training for this kind of situation. The driver gave no thought to the feelings of the woman, or the anger of the other passengers who were being delayed. No one at the company had thought about what to do when things go wrong. No one empowered the driver to make a decision to satisfy the customer. This driver claimed he had worked for the company for three years.

The driver and young lady continued to argue, with the driver getting more belligerent with each remark. I had to intervene. I told him in, a nice way, to stop being rude to the lady. He countered rudely, "Shut up, I'm in control here." By the time we got back to the shuttle terminal, all the passengers were yelling at the driver. He jumped out of the van, and put his fists up to fight with the twelve men on board. We just broke out laughing at the absurdity of it all!

As we talked in the van, I told the other people we can't accept this ludicrous situation. I led a revolt. I said we were going back inside to talk to the shuttle manager, and demand another driver. We all piled out, opened the back door of the van, retrieved our luggage, and went to the manager. When we explained the situation to the manager, the driver was fired on the spot. It was three hours after my flight arrived before they found a new driver and delivered me to my hotel.

The shuttle company needed to do three things to prevent that situation. First, get better at hiring the drivers. Second, train them in courtesy with passengers. Third, empower them to make decisions to satisfy the customer, not enrage them. Think of how many times the passengers will tell this story. I've told hundreds of people already. Again, a reputation is ruined because of a lack of proper hiring, training, and empowering.

Share Information

Employees tell us in surveys that they want to know where and how they fit in. They want to know that they are a vital cog and not just someone putting in their time. They want to know what the big picture is, and what their relationship is to it. The only way you can make them feel an important part of what is going on is to share as much information as possible.

By letting people know where the company is at financially, and where they are headed, you let them know they are important. Tell them how they are doing in relationship to sales projections. Let them know what the economic climate is like. Have them understand the balance sheet, and how it relates to them and their department.

Share individual and group performance data. This is one way to let them know there is a relationship between what they do, how they do it, and how the entire company does.

Finally, share the changes ahead that will affect the quality of their everyday worklife. Tell them which direction the company is headed. Let them know about new products and technology. Tell them as soon as possible. Otherwise you only feed rumors.

Respect People's Differences

With the workforce changing in so many ways, people come in a multitude of colors and languages. They come from a multitude of backgrounds. Therefore their perceptions, work styles, and methods of getting things done are going to be different. Their skill base and ways of going about their everyday work will vary. But, different doesn't mean better or worse compared to someone else.

Why do some managers think there is only one way of doing things? Many times there is no one best way; no method that is perfect for everyone who does it. The best method is the method that is employed by a worker and gets the best results.

For people to be empowered, they have to use the methods that are appropriate to them in the context of their background. As managers and owners, you have to give them the freedom to be themselves. When possible, let them choose their own path, as long as they are meeting the standards set and are contributing to total customer satisfaction.

It is interesting that when people use their own discretion and are able to do things in a way they deem appropriate, they frequently exceed expectations and standards. The way they got there, or their means to an end is the only difference. Accept and respect people for whom they are!

Not all foreign born Americans will readily adopt the concept of empowerment. In order to empower workers, it's also necessary to understand their attitudes about authority.

Many come from cultures where the older male is the boss. These bosses are autocratic and authoritarian. They make the rules, and everyone else must obey them. They create all the decisions and pass them down. No one makes a move until the orders are given. No matter what orders are given, the boss is never questioned nor judged. In some Asiatic countries, the subordinates are taught to not even make eye contact with the boss.

This makes it hard for some of the foreign born to accept empowerment, involvement, and participation. They find the concept that the boss wants and values their opinion difficult to comprehend. They often will make a wrong conclusion when they are asked.

A vice president told me a story about one of his competitors in a blue-collar industry. The majority of the people working for him were male Puerto Ricans. They were used to the idea that the boss told them what to do, and they just did it.

However, one day the boss decided to ask them their opinion about a particular problem he was having. The workers started to avoid him, and some of them quit. He couldn't understand what was happening. After some investigation, he was shocked to learn that his innocent attempt to get people involved was interpreted as a sign that the company was in trouble. The employees reasoned that if you ask me my opinion, you don't know what to do.

If you don't know what to do, the company must be going out of business. Therefore, we should start looking for another job! The point is that the more you understand about the diversity of today's workforce, the more you will be successful in managing them.

Empowerment does work. It is a successful method of improving performance, service, and quality, as well as employee job satisfaction. But, like any new, permanent change you attempt, there must be a strong commitment from the top, that spreads to all levels of management. Without the initiative, involvement, and encouragement from top management, it will just be another passing trend.

Quick Chapter Tips

1. To empower employees, eliminate fears; especially the fear of making mistakes.

2. Remove the barriers or policies and procedures that prevent employees from making decisions or solving problems for customers.

3. Hire diverse, creative people who can come up with unique solutions. A diverse workforce brings a wealth of perspectives and different points of view.

4. Train your workforce well so they will be empowered to make intelligent decisions.

5. Share as much information with employees as possible about your organization's direction and economic outlook, and how they fit into the picture. Let them know they are an important part of your organization's success.

6. Realize that the way they come to a solution is not the issue. More importantly, it is solving the problem to satisfy the customer. Give people the freedom to be themselves.

Teamwork: Working Together to Achieve Outstanding Service

Long ago, our pioneering ancestors discovered the power of teamwork. By harnessing horses into teams, they were able to reach new destinations, going farther then ever before. Many successful companies today have been able to harness their workforce into teams and are forging ahead to become the progressive leaders in their industries. In the future, team effectiveness will be one of the keys to ensuring customer satisfaction and total quality management.

Benefits of Teams

Having functioning, effective teams in your organization gives you the freedom to tend to other issues. You can manage your time better. Within the framework of an effective team, employees take control and get the job done.

Also, your entire organization will function much more smoothly. This is because when people communicate better they eliminate barriers to productivity and performance. People work together towards common goals rather than being strictly out for themselves. This builds commitment. Higher productivity, increased efficiency, and greater effectiveness will result.

Effective teams ensure your organization higher levels of quality and customer service. A level of innovation and excellence is achieved that is impossible to reach when working independent of one another. The continuous search for improvement reduces errors, mistakes, and defects. Teams work harder together at solving customer problems because they have a common sense of purpose and are more creative. Because of this, team members have greater job satisfaction.

When your people work well together as a team, there is less stress. Tensions are decreased between individuals. This in turn leads to increased morale, greater enthusiasm, and higher energy levels while lateness, absenteeism, and turnover are reduced. The team members become stronger as individuals and as a unit. As J.C. Penny once said, "The five separate fingers are five independent units. Close them and a fist multiplies strength. This is organization."

Characteristics of Effective Teams and Teamwork

A team is very similar to a family. Leo Tolstoy said so eloquently, "All happy families resemble one another, but each unhappy family is unhappy in its own way." The ones that are happy all have the same characteristics.

In my management seminars on "Teamwork and Team play," I lead a brainstorming exercise on effective teams and their characteristics. I found the following characteristics showed up again and again. Successful teams all resemble one another. They all have similarities that are seen in every industry, and in all workers.

Effective Team Leadership

An effective team leader has a different function than that of a traditional manager or boss. In the past, a manager controlled and directed his team. Now the team leader makes decisions in light of the team structure and goals. You, as a team leader, become a coach, supporter, provider, and facilitator to the team. With these skills, a climate is created within which the team will function.

An old Chinese proverb says:

"If you want one year of prosperity, grow grain.
If you want ten years of prosperity, grow trees.
If you want one hundred years of prosperity,
grow people."

In order to grow people, learn to vary your leadership style for the situation at hand, and learn to work with each individual team member. Take the time to develop team members in order to get the most out of each individual. *Effective team leaders get ordinary people to accomplish extraordinary achievements.*

If you were growing a flower garden, you would certainly spend a lot of time with those plants that needed more care. You wouldn't treat each plant exactly the same. Some would need more water, more sunlight, and more fertilizer. Some would need more tender, loving care. It's the same with your people.

You are the formal leader of your department or company. However, if your people are to begin thinking and working as a team, you won't be successful if you are always leading alone. The leadership has to be shared at times among employees that are part of that team. All team members need to take some of the responsibility to move the team along the path to its common goal.

You won't be there every minute to assume a leadership role. There are critical times when leadership is needed by your team members. They often need to take the responsibility to initiate an action or solve a problem on their own. This requires training, open communication, and empowerment of employees to make decisions.

An effective team leader can see the possibilities that others cannot. They are usually thinking ahead of the team. As Charles Garfield says in his well known book, *Peak Performers,* they "anticipate, adapt, and act." They can look over any difficult situation, make changes in their leadership style, and find unconventional solutions to problems. They are not limited by doing things the way they were always done. They are not hindered by the constraints of the past.

Common Goals

In 1962, President John F. Kennedy made a commitment, he set a goal to have a man on the moon by the end of the decade. He put into motion the development of a plan, whose one sole purpose was to land on the moon within a specific deadline. The people in the space industry ranked all other projects secondary. They were all united around one purpose, one goal, and one mission. As a result the mission was successful.

All effective teams are characterized by having one or more common goals. They have a clearly defined purpose. In an organization, this goal can be 100% customer satisfaction, zero customer complaints, or zero defects. No matter what the goals are, they are specific, clearly understood, and readily accepted by all the team members. Members are committed to those goals.

A goal should be obtainable and measurable. That means goals can't be set so high that the team is doomed to fail, and becomes frustrated and cynical. The goals have to be flexible in case they need revision. Progress towards the goal is continually monitored. Feedback is given that educates and motivates the team toward their goals. Just as people crave individual feedback, team members want to know how they are doing as a team. Without measuring the progress, you can't let people know whether they are successful. Teams need to track and determine if they have satisfied customer expectations.

One of the difficulties in achieving team goals is that people have to often overlook their own personal goals. It is a great challenge to assist your people to achieve their own individual goals, but keep them within the framework of the team. Personal goals should be defined within the context of the team.

The team's goals must come first. When the personal goals become more important than the team's, the team will not achieve their goals. Behaviors become adversarial. These adversarial behaviors lead to power struggles. People try to beat each other out. Winning at all costs becomes paramount. Others who are not interested in getting their own way cope by withdrawing and just doing the bare minimum.

When coach Jimmy Johnson was at the University of Miami, he had a slogan during the year he lead the team to a National Championship. That slogan was "Big Team, Little Me." Players were constantly reminded to put their egos aside. He asked them to forget about their own individual fame and glory. He wanted them to work for the one team goal of winning the National Championship.

If you look at many of the professional football and basketball teams over the years, you'll see that few of them are champions more than once. After that first win, individual goals of fame, money, endorsements, and appearances often become the priority. The team's goals become secondary. Individuals find it difficult to concentrate on the team's goal of winning.

When teams develop their goals, it's critical that they decide on the correct behaviors expected from each member. Be sure your people fully understand the ways they will treat each other, or the house rules by which they will live.

One effective exercise I use in my teambuilding seminars is to have groups of people brainstorm the following areas:

- An effective team member exhibits the following behaviors toward other team members . . .

- An effective team member never exhibits the following behaviors toward other team members . . .

- When there is a problem or conflict between team members, we take the following steps to correct the situation . . .

Next, I have each group relate to the others what they decided, and by consensus we create a master list of these areas and give each a copy. All participants then pledge to abide by them.

Clear and Accepted Roles

Would you knowingly have heart surgery with a team of doctors and nurses who did not know exactly what their roles were during the operation? Would you land a fighter jet, (if you knew how), loaded with fuel and missiles on a nuclear-powered aircraft carrier if each team member wasn't performing their role to exact pre-set standards? These questions may be absurd, and the answers obvious, but they point out an important fact about effective teams.

A key element in effective teams is that each member understands their individual role as part of the team. In order to understand their role, everyone must understand each job task. All members should know how to perform those tasks, and what is expected as a final result. They should know that they will be held accountable.

When roles are not clear, some people will repeat tasks that others are doing. Some people may not do what they are supposed to and gaps will result. Conflict ensues. Morale is lowered. Goals are not achieved.

In some cases, team members may know their own role, but they don't understand how it fits in with the rest of the team. It makes the quality level of the entire team suffer.

A good example of this is a client of mine who brought me in to trouble shoot a problem they were having. This small business repaired brakes on heavy duty vehicles, and had instituted quality teams in their company. They felt productivity would go up; they could service more vehicles and be more profitable.

The role of each person within the three person teams was not clearly defined. As a result, the team members didn't communicate some important information to each other. They didn't think it impacted the other members.

Consequently, the brakes weren't being reassembled properly. Some critical parts were left out, and some work was done twice. Productivity had dropped instead of increasing.

Fortunately, we discovered the problem before a tragedy occurred. This is an example of what can happen when the exact role of each team member isn't clear.

With effective teams, what is expected has been defined, communicated, and reinforced. Members understand each behavior and skill required, and exactly how it must be performed. They understand how their roles affect each other. They support each other in those roles. Standards can't be so rigid that they stifle individual creativity, empowerment, or decision making. Team leaders and members need to know when to be flexible.

Cooperation

When employees cooperate, they are working together simultaneously to achieve common goals. In your organization, that goal could be outstanding service. People who cooperate realize that they can't achieve that common goal unless they collaborate effectively. They share a mutual fate: either success or failure. They give of themselves to others, and they expect to get the same in return. They expect everyone to carry their own weight and pull together.

When team members don't get that cooperation returned, the mutual goal won't be achieved. When competition, rather than cooperation, becomes the norm, the goal can't be reached. People who spend all their time and energy competing with one another have very little left for cooperation.

People who cooperate share information readily, exchange resources and ideas, and have constructive disagreements. They mutually support each other, with back pats and high-fives. An emotional bond develops that glues the team together. People who compete usually hold back information or use it to take advantage of others. The disagreements are bitter and only create undue tension and stress.

How do you determine if your team members are cooperating? Start by asking a lot of questions. You can do this one-on-one, in group discussions, or by a survey. The answers will help you to assess and analyze where cooperation is lacking, or competition is cropping up. Here are some questions that will point you in the right direction:

- Do we work toward common goals and objectives?
- Are communications open enough to achieve those goals?
- Are we able to disagree without causing anger and resentment?

- Do we respond to each other's needs?
- Do we share our priorities?
- Do we resolve difficulties through open discussions?
- Do team members have mutual respect for each other?

These questions and the ensuing discussions should help you realize the level of cooperation that exists in your team.

Another benefit of cooperation is that it leads to better internal service between team members, different teams, and other departments. Your people must realize that each employee and department is a customer of one another. Cooperation is crucial in achieving any high level of internal service. Cooperation enables other individuals to get the resources and information they need in a timely manner.

One way to bring awareness of the importance of cooperation to everyone is to have every employee and department answer the following three questions:

1. What individuals rely on my (our) cooperation and service?

2. How or why do they depend on my (our) cooperation and service?

3. How can I (we) cooperate better to ensure these people are being well served?

By answering these questions, people become more aware of how important cooperation is. In addition, these answers motivate people to make a commitment to cooperate and give better internal service.

Discuss the answers at departmental or team meetings. Feedback from other employees and teams will let you know if you are on target. Your employees will become more aware of the interdependence that certain individuals or groups have on each other. This can only increase internal service, and having better internal service means better service for your customers.

Synergy

Vince Lombardi, the great, late coach of the Green Bay Packers said, "The achievements of an organization are the results of the combined efforts of each individual." Effective teams combine those individual efforts and achieve a level of synergy. Synergy means that the whole is greater than the sum of it parts. Team members obtain strength from each other. They achieve a level of energy and enthusiasm that is impossible to achieve alone. Your people may be good as individuals, but working well together sends them to new levels of greatness. They become like a heat-seeking missile, moving along towards its target. *Nothing can stop them from success.*

When teams achieve a level of high energy, that energy becomes self-perpetuating and contagious. Team members enjoy operating at that level and strive to maintain it. There is an atmosphere of excitement and a feeling that together, they can conquer anything. When there is failure, they recognize it. However, failure is looked upon simply as a stepping stone, not a roadblock. Members learn from the experience, correct the process, and then move on.

The team leader is the one who sets the tone and climate and gets people excited. The leader makes his or her people feel like winners. They recognize progress, achievement, and attempts at achievement.

The leader has that unique ability to see the entire playing field and is able to extend the game plan into the future. They are visionaries. They understand what the end result should look like.

He or she also recognizes that achieving all the team's goals won't come easy. They are able to foresee the roadblocks ahead. However, they solve those challenges early on and keep the team on track. They are able to maintain the synergy.

In 1972, when the Miami Dolphins were the only team ever to go undefeated, with a record of 17-0, they had achieved a level of synergy that may be impossible to achieve again. Don Shula was able to take unknown players, many of whom were unwanted by other teams, and have them work together at an unprecedented level. He knew how to blend the players to the team's best advantage. He had ordinary players perform at an extraordinary level.

Team members gained a strength and energy from each other that couldn't be realized on their own. Each player had a deep understanding of one another's responsibilities, as well as their own. They knew that they had a unity of purpose; one that was higher than their individual purpose.

Coach Shula had them concentrate each week only on the game immediately ahead. They looked upon each game as a challenge and a stepping stone. Each week the coach got the team up to face the challenge. Each week they achieved that magic level of synergy.

Commitment

Commitment is a spark that fosters creativity. It acts like a fuel that fan the flames of energy. It wields the team into action. It creates a cohesive group. *Commitment enables team members to find a way to achieve their goals.*

In order for a team to be successful, the members must have a high level of commitment to the team concept. This means they give their belief, support, and time to the team. They supply the energy to achieve the teams goals and objectives. Members feel it's worthwhile.

In order for commitment to exist, there has to be an atmosphere of trust. Team leaders and members have to do what they said they are going to do, within the manner and time frame they said they will do it.

People will only trust when they know there is honesty and fairness. The honesty may not always be what people want to hear, but it's often what they need to hear. Being open is critical to creating trust.

Fairness can only be achieved when there is consistency in actions. You can't have one set of policies for one individual and not for others. Although policies should be flexible, they can't be changed with every whim. Team leaders need to be honest and fair, in spite of the obstacles that often block these behaviors.

Commitment also means that subteams or small cliques can't be formed. This often happens when two or three individuals have a common interest that naturally draws them together, or collectively they disagree with the team's objectives. Team members who are committed to the team concept are effective in helping, supporting, and nurturing other team members. They help members who are having problems with some aspect of their work or home life. They listen to each other, counsel each other, and lend a helping hand.

There can be a negative side to this type of commitment. Team members can become subjective in their decision making. They may tend to avoid advice from those outside the team. This may lead to a "groupthink" situation where quality and service are sacrificed due to a sense of obligation. "As teams become closer, they support one another's positions in conflicts—perhaps whether or not their colleagues are in the right. It is easy to see how blind commitment could undermine the quality of a team's work" (Francis & Young, 1992, p. 84).

Open Communication and Feedback

Effective team members are truly interested in information that is relevant to the everyday workflow and the solving of daily customer problems and challenges. Information that is needed is readily given out and readily received. Ideas are listened to and are not ridiculed. People share ideas candidly. Creativity is encouraged, not stifled. Customers are not only served better, but they are also served faster.

This honest, open communication also has trust as its foundation. When people feel valued, they trust others; and when they trust others, they openly communicate. They feel they can be truthful. They don't worry about being punished for their honesty.

An atmosphere of openness is one where not only information is exchanged, but also feelings. Feedback between members expresses both content and emotions. When corrective information is shared, it helps to develop people. When people share feelings, it creates closer relationships. Team members bond together. When they share both, *it creates that magic synergy.*

The difficult part of sharing feelings is that some people do not express feelings in a way that is helpful, while others aren't use to getting feedback that expresses feelings. The feedback can bring on embarrassment or be very damaging to a person. It can even create a "threatened" feeling in some people.

When there is too much praising, and not enough corrective feedback, people can start to believe they are near-perfect. They can become complacent. If everyone is near-perfect all the time, it's a red flag that standards have been set too low.

For communication and feedback to be effective with a team (unlike individual feedback), there needs to be a blend of both the positive and negative. This blend has a more energizing and bonding effect. People are excited about what they did right, and they become determined to correct what they did wrong.

Train your people on how to give each other feedback and how to make necessary changes afterwards. Have them learn to objectively analyze and assess how they performed as individuals and as a team. After a negative assessment is made, then determine why it was negative. Then correct the process or implement a new one.

The purpose of team communication and feedback is never to blame, only to learn and improve. The challenge for any team is to take its failures, communicate them in a manner so that team members remain positive, and then move on to making positive change.

Comraderie

Vince Lombardi in a speech to the American Management Association said, "Love is loyalty. Love is teamwork. Love is a deep respect for the individual. Heart power is the strength of your company." With effective teams, people get to know and like each other. Respect between team members becomes critical. They feel that they can rely on one another to get things done. Team members develop a team spirit that encourages, shares, supports, and nurtures. *They value each other.*

While effective teams work hard together, they also play hard together outside of work. Sponsoring company picnics, sports teams, or allowing employees to work together on a community project goes a long way towards establishing personal relationships. Employees can build a better bond when they are involved together outside the workplace. It also lessens the stress of everyday challenges.

Friendly Disagreement

Obviously, team members aren't always in agreement with each other. Some disagreement is a sign of a healthy team. If people are agreeing all the time, this stifles creativity and judgment. Effective team members challenge each other, yet are open with each other.

People interacting all day will always produce conflict. However, this conflict needs to be worked out in a healthy manner. People need to express their differences and not sweep them under the rug. People tend to avoid each other when there is conflict. Sometimes they become silently resentful or openly hostile. This only leads to decreased productivity, more errors, and customer service suffers.

Consider having a rule or procedure in place when angry situations arise. One way that works is to have the angry employee discuss the situation with a team leader or manager, and then have the situation solved by the entire team.

Another helpful method we found to eliminate conflict involves sitting both parties down, and questioning each one individually while the other person listens. Varney lists the following helpful questions for resolving disagreements:

1. What is the problem as you perceive it?
2. What does the other person do that contributes to the problem?
3. What do you want or need from the other person?
4. What do you do that contributes to the problem?

5. What first step can you take to resolve the problem? (Varney, 1989, p.76)

Team Problem Solving

Robert Townsend, the former President of Avis Car Rental, stated that decisions he made individually only had a success rate of just over 50%. However, when he sat down with his staff to solve the problems together, the success rate was much greater (Varney, 1989). The richness of different people with different thought processes, and different levels of creativity greatly enhances your prospects of achieving a greater solution.

The following method of solving problems is one which I have frequently used during my seminars. It is one that can be used with your team, in a variety of situations, customer related or not.

- Get team members to define the exact problem.

- Brainstorm for the real causes versus the symptoms. It is necessary to keep asking why, again and again, until members get to the root cause.

- Generate a number of possible solutions because the first solution is not necessarily the best.

- Decide on the best possible solution. Keep in mind costs versus benefits.

- Create a step-by-step plan to implement the solution.

- Implement the solution. Monitor and measure the changes to see that the problem has been solved.

Strategies for Team Leaders

Top management's role is critical to creating an atmosphere of teamwork. Leaders start the initiative in creating the team. They send the message about the importance of teams. They communicate that teamwork is an integral part of the organization's culture and everyday tasks.

The following are some guidelines that will help you in creating a productive, well-oiled team.

Create a Vision

Begin by creating a vision with your employees and promote that vision again and again. The vision has to be exciting and uplifting. It has to stretch everyone's imagination of what can be, not just what is. What does an organization that has world class service look like? How do world class service employees function together as a team?

A vision must inspire! In order to inspire it can't be too far-fetched. To be believed, it has be grounded in reality. A difficult vision is challenging. An impossible vision is demotivating. Employees have to find it meaningful. It should be significant to each team member on a personal level.

When Jan Carlzon, of Scandinavian Airlines, turned the company around in the early 1980s, he created a vision for the future. He redefined the airline as a European businessperson's airline, with a service level to surpass all others in the industry.

He created his vision by knowing what the customer wanted. He reasoned that if his people gave the customer what they wanted during each "Moment of Truth" or customer contact they would be very successful. He communicated the vision to his people and put his plan into action. Today, SAS's success story has become almost legendary throughout the world.

Model Team Behaviors

Sparky Anderson, Manager of the Detroit Tigers, said "You don't become a leader because you say you are. It's more of what you do than what you say." As a manager, you need to role model what a team player and leader should be. Show your members that you too are a part of the entire team. This means managers must exhibit all the positive characteristics of a team player, in addition to the characteristics of a leader.

You have to make decisions that show you are willing to stick to what you say. Sometimes, these decisions are very unpopular to the team. When Joe Namath was in his junior year of college at the University of Alabama, he broke a team rule. He was out partying the night before a big game and had a little too much to drink.

Even though they had two big games left, Coach Bear Bryant told Joe he broke the rules and was off the team. The Bear knew it would be tough to win without Joe. But, he realized he had to lay down the law, no matter how unpopular. The fans and alumni howled in anger. The Bear received thousands of letters and phone calls of protest. He never wavered for a moment. The Crimson Tide barely won the next two games.

The following year, the Bear let Joe back on the team, and they went on to win the National Championship. Years later, Joe admitted in retrospect, it was right for the Bear to do what he did.

Implement Team-Based Strategies

Leaders develop the strategies and implement the systems that make teamwork a critical part of each work day. Leaders set standards for team behaviors and communicate and train those standards to everyone. They give feedback and use coaching sessions to reinforce the team message. Leaders include team behaviors as part of the overall performance appraisal process. They make teamwork a criteria for promotion.

Develop Team Incentives

You need to make teamwork, teamplay, cooperation, and internal service all part of an incentive and reward system. Team players' skills can be used as one basis for bonuses and rewards. Develop a program of team rewards. Give a "Most Valuable Player" award to the one steady, consistent team player who often goes above and beyond. Publicly recognize team behaviors. Finally, let unproductive teams know that as a team, they are held accountable for their failures.

Managing Diverse Teams to Give Outstanding Service

Having an effective, well-oiled team that will serve your customers well is a real challenge. When you have diverse people from different genders, races, languages, and ethnic backgrounds, it compounds the matter.

Diversity issues in the workplace can be a double-edged sword. Cliques and rivalries based on ethnic background or race can paralyze teamwork. This can lead to suspicion and open hostility that can keep groups from being productive. This in-fighting only serves to prevent people from satisfying the customer.

On the other hand, this diversity can also stimulate effective problem solving and creative solutions when people value each other's differences, beliefs, and ideas. For this to take place, the right atmosphere where people are able to discuss their differences needs to be created. Diverse people need to be able to sit down, and lay their differences on the table. People should be able to voice their opinions and integrate them into customer-oriented solutions.

Here are some suggestions that will help you manage service with a diverse team:

Model the Correct Behavior

I have said before how critical it is to be a role model of the service behaviors that you want employees to exhibit. It is also imperative to model the behaviors that support a diverse team. This may involve simply talking about the value of diversity, and the business reasons that make it so important.

It may mean taking an active role in the elimination of discrimination. Be proactive in recruiting and hiring of diverse people for your team. Eliminate cultural biases in the performance standards. Enable team members to break through promotional barriers regardless of their differences. Reward and recognize each individual in a way that is meaningful to them.

Don't Fake it

Too often, people from diverse backgrounds are approached by people that act like they really care about them. They fake wanting to know about their culture. They often have their own private agenda, and people see through this. The only thing that this accomplishes is the erosion of the ability to work together. Be sure to be genuine in your approach to managing diverse employees.

Find Common Ground

Common ground is defined as a "shared set of assumptions that provide the basis for a cooperative action" (Loden & Rosener, 1991, p. 138). There has to be some commonly accepted principles that employees will go by. For this to happen, people have to share the vision created by top management. They also must share the values, goals, priorities, expectations, commitments, and rewards. Every team member should have a purpose common to the team. All people should believe in the value of providing outstanding service.

Understand How Others Think

Again, keep in mind, different groups have different backgrounds which create different ways of doing things. There is no right way vs. wrong way, but just a different way. The more your people understand the thought process and behaviors of people who are different, the more sensitive they will be. That means paying attention to people's values, beliefs, and the way they think. This is the only way the differences can be truly appreciated.

Realize There Will Be Culture Clashes

Even homogeneous teams have many conflicts. Diverse teams are bound to have more conflicts as a result of their differences. There is going to be a clash of basic values and attitudes. Loden and Rosener define culture clash as a "conflict over basic values that occurs between groups of people with different core identities" (Loden & Rosener, p.

121). One group usually believes their way is the right way, and that people who disagree will just have to learn that their way is the correct way.

Just anticipating the clashes is the first step in moving toward finding a common ground. An effective leader can foresee potential time bombs and work with individuals or groups to diffuse them.

If you have tried to implement a team structure in your workplace and it hasn't worked, or if you are in the midst of doing so and it isn't working, go back and start again by:

- Articulating the vision you created for the direction you want your teams to go.

- Reviewing the characteristics of teamwork. Assess and analyze your staff in those areas to see if the characteristics exist and to what degree. Use these characteristics as a basis for discussions at a meeting. Ask questions such as:

    1. Do we work together as a team toward common goals?

    2. Are the communications open enough to achieve those goals?

    3. Are we able to disagree with each other without causing anger and resentment?

These questions should help you and your staff to realize the strengths and weaknesses of your team. The only way to get better is to assess where you are presently with where you want to be. Then, plan the changes and institute them. Monitor the changes to be sure you are successful. And one more thing: start by having your team involved in planning the changes that need to be made!

Quick Chapter Tips

1. Team leaders are coaches, supporters, providers, and facilitators to a team. Effective team leaders get ordinary people to do extraordinary things.

2. Effective teams have common goals. The goals are obtainable, measurable, and flexible. The team's goals come before the individual team member's goals.

3. A key element in effective teamwork is that each member understands their role as part of the team and each other's roles as well. They understand how their roles affect each other.

4. Cooperation is a vital key to the success of a team. Team members who cooperate share information, resources, ideas, and mutually support one another. Cooperation leads to better internal service and better service for customers.

5. Team members gain strength and energy from each other. When they are functioning at peak performance they achieve synergy. This synergy happens when members have a unity of purpose that is higher than their own purpose.

6. Commitment from team members enables them to achieve their goals. A high level of honesty and fairness has to exist for team members to trust each other, and commit to the team.

7. A team that is successful will have members who feel valued, who trust one another, and can openly communicate in a truthful manner. Information and feelings are shared and team members bond together.

8. Successful team leaders create a vision that inspires. They exhibit all the positive characteristics of a team player. Leaders set the standards for team behaviors, and communicate and train those standards to everyone. They develop an incentive and reward system.

9. Having team members from different races, ethnic backgrounds, and of different genders can either stimulate or create problems for a team. To avoid conflict, team leaders need to be active in eliminating discrimination and be genuine in relating to diverse members.

10. Team members need to understand the thought processes and behaviors of members who are different from themselves.

The Art of Giving High Quality Feedback

How many times have you said the wrong thing to one of your employees, only to regret the words later? Many times, managers and owners see an employee giving service incorrectly, and they react emotionally, only to end up with an angry and defensive employee.

How can you find a better way to say what you need to say? How can you say things in a productive manner so that your staff can correct the behavior, and do a better job serving your customers? And, when they are doing things right, how can you reinforce those service behaviors so they continue doing the right things?

One thing missing in many organizations is a continuous flow of information to make people aware of how they are doing, and if they are achieving their service goals. This information is the link between a job description and a performance evaluation. This connection is called high quality feedback. It's a response to the basic human desire of all employees to know how they are doing. It's also a critical management skill because it reinforces or corrects performance.

Owners and managers often give feedback about service performance without really thinking about what they are saying, or the effects of their statements. Some never give any feedback at all. They hold it in until there is a problem. Or, they save all the errors and problems for a once a year, during evaluations. Then they nail employees to the wall. This kind of feedback only creates mediocrity, excuses, blaming, and poor service.

Different Needs of a Changing Workforce

With today's workforce being so diverse, it's necessary to be sensitive to the feedback requirements of different people. The young American born workforce craves feedback all the time. They are insulted and hurt very easily by outright criticism. They almost don't care how something is said, as long as it's positive. Above all, they don't want to go unnoticed (see Chapter Three).

Foreign born Americans are not used to the typical, direct way American managers discuss performance. In many of their native countries, feedback is given in an indirect manner. Each culture has its own unique way of giving feedback. Often an employer will only give subtle hints about performance not being adequate. What is most important to some foreign borns is saving face. Saving face is related to saving self-esteem. This is more important to them than how they perform. One key is, whenever possible, to learn how that particular culture gives feedback.

Having your respect is critical to a foreign born's productivity. Public criticism is enough to make them never come back to work. They may never complain about the criticism. They just don't show up the next day. Private criticism is enough to have them avoid any contact with you from then on.

Many foreign borns won't ask how they are doing or how to do things better. They will never ask questions if they don't understand. If they perceive that you think they don't understand, it threatens their self-esteem. They suffer humiliation. You have to take the time to show them how American management methods are different. You need to teach them that feedback is critical to success. This can go a long way towards eliminating feedback problems.

When giving corrective feedback to workers who don't speak English, do it in private. The ideal method is to have another employee who speaks their language give them the feedback. Since you can't hire a full time trainer who speaks many different languages, consider using an employee who is bilingual to assist in giving feedback. This may be best if it's done one on one, without you.

If you are the one giving the feedback, let that employee know, very precisely, what you expect from them. If there is a language barrier, talk slowly, with short words and sentences. Repeat frequently, and be sure you are not using slang or company jargon they can't understand. If you have to, physically show them the wrong method they used, and then show them the better way. Be sure they understand which is which. Smile and be warm and sincere. Use positive phrases and positive tones. Encourage them and let them know that you have faith in them.

Be careful not to put your hands on foreign born people when talking. This is taboo in some countries. Americans, as a group, are fairly warm. We tend to touch a lot. We do a lot of back and shoulder patting. People from Asiatic and South American countries may find this very embarrassing or humiliating. Learn to keep your distance. *The more you know about the values and attitudes about a particular culture, the easier it is to give them feedback and motivate them.*

Know Right from Wrong

When you want to change performance, there is a right and a wrong way to give feedback that applies to all cultures and employees. The right way enhances performance, increases productivity, and changes negative behavior. When employees receive this kind of feedback, it is almost inevitable they will make some change to improve. It provides people with the insight and direction that intrinsically motivates. Ken Blanchard, author of the *One-Minute Manager*, hits it right on the mark when he states, "feedback is the breakfast of champions."

The wrong way is nothing but criticism. It creates distrust, conflict, absenteeism, sabotage, and eventual turnover. It damages morale throughout the organization. Employees spend most of the day feeling outraged. They wonder "what makes you so perfect?" or "what birthright do you have?" The sad part is that it creates serious damage without correcting the negative behavior. In addition, your customers suffer. *Employees will treat the customer only as well as they are treated by those who manage them.*

If giving feedback is a motivator and dramatically improves performance, then it is not a skill to be taken lightly. It takes time, thought, and preparation. It will only flourish in the right kind of positive, supportive environment. It will only work when the feedback creates a learning situation instead of a blast of negative comments. Like any other skill, you can develop it if you work at it.

Set the Stage

To give high quality feedback, first set the service goals, service standards of behavior, and the house rules. *If employees don't know exactly what behaviors you expect, then any behavior is okay.* If they aren't told how they are doing, then they assume they are doing things right. If they don't understand what good or excellent performance versus substandard or non-performance looks like, then they can't provide it. If they don't know what it takes to make their manager happy, they can't. Tie feedback into specific service standards and service related goals that are repeatedly communicated (see Chapter Five).

Remember: what gets written down gets done, and can be managed and measured. This gives you a basis for feedback and recognition. And, everyone will be working from the same page. If your performance standards or service goals are sitting somewhere in a three-ring binder, it's time to dust them off and use them.

Goals are just a wish until you clearly write them out and assign a deadline date to them. Deadlines create a sense of urgency. People forget goals and standards very quickly after a meeting that only discusses them. They go back to work at a fast and furious pace, and their mind shifts to getting things done; not how to do them correctly.

Writing out goals and standards serves as a blueprint. It gives everyone a set of rules to go by. You wouldn't build a brand new house without having the blueprints drawn up by an architect. Nor would the contractor start building without those blueprints. Likewise, you can't have your employees exhibiting standards and achieving goals unless they have the blueprint or plan.

If you are going to write out standards and goals, then you need to find a way to keep score. Everyone wants to know how they are doing. Every sport keeps score of how each team is doing. Athletes get detailed records in many different categories that tells them how they performed. Rock stars, musicians and other performers keep track of records sold, concert tickets bought, and where they are on the charts.

So too, your people need to know their score. They want to compare their performance to the goals set, or to the goals they achieved before. They need to see improvement, or where improvement is needed and why. "In Workplace 2000 measurement will become the primary vehicle for communicating business strategy to employees, for triggering recognition of good performance, and for supporting employee problem-solving efforts" (Boyett & Conn, pp. 65-66).

Deal with problems that are within the control of the employee and can be changed. If employees don't have all the necessary equipment, tools, or resources to do their job, this is a managerial or operations problem, not a situation for giving feedback. Faulty training or lack of training, particularly with new people, can also be the cause of the problem (see Chapter Six).

Finally, remember it's critical that an employee maintains dignity and self-respect. If not, resentment and anger will surely rear their ugly heads. That means providing feedback can't be taken lightly. Too much hinges on it. *You have to think about it before you give it.*

Timing Is Everything

Give feedback as soon as possible. The sooner your staff receives feedback, the easier it is for them to change the behavior. Boyett and Conn have determined that, "in Workplace 2000, feedback will be monthly, weekly, daily, and in some cases hourly, or even instantaneously" (Boyett & Conn, p.77).

Sometimes it may even require pulling someone off a job to correct a situation. It is much better to correct it immediately, than have an employee make the same mistake throughout the day. If you wait too long, you tend to minimize or forget the situation. Service and quality can only suffer.

Certainly, when an emergency or safety violation occurs, you need to give feedback instantaneously. This is also true when an employee is breaking a law, industry regulation, or company rule.

One method I created for companies I consulted with involves drawing up a list of ten to twenty key, measurable service standards, written out clearly, to be easily understood by all employees. At the top of the list we have three categories for managers to check off. They are: unsatisfactory, satisfactory, and exceptional. You can use other terms, but these were ones those employees decided upon. These categories also equalled a number, with one being unsatisfactory, two being satisfactory, and three being exceptional.

Each week the managers check off the boxes and add up the score for that week. This requires managers observing their employees frequently. It may seem as if there isn't enough time to do this. Managers need to remember what the basic job is of management. *It is to help people to do what they are required to do.* Managers can't help people succeed if they aren't observing employees to see if they are performing correctly.

The employees like the idea of getting weekly scores. It helps them to stay on course, and correct minor deficiencies before they become major. It enables them to achieve the goals set before the deadlines.

When you are not sure of the circumstances or behavior, never give immediate feedback. This is especially true when you have second hand information or hearsay.

Another time to delay feedback is when the employee has just dealt with an irate customer or had a conflict with another employee. At this point, the employee is angry or hurt, and it doesn't do any good for you to add fuel to the fire. Wait until they have calmed down before you approach them.

Be sensitive. If an employee is already under tremendous pressure or stress, hold off. At this point, they will be less receptive anyway. In all situations, weigh the pluses against the minuses and make your decision accordingly.

Pick the Right Place

The worse thing you can do is give negative feedback within earshot of someone else! Be sensitive to the discomfort or embarrassment this creates. If customers are present, take the employee aside to correct the problem. If other employees are near, hold off your comments until you get a moment to speak to the employee alone. Privacy and confidentiality can be critical to accepting the feedback. Only resentment will result from humiliation.

Don't allow interruptions to your discussion. You want to create a good climate to allow for better understanding. This also sends a message to the employee that they are important, and their job performance really matters to you.

Cool Down

How you say things is as important as when you say things. You may be upset or angry about the situation. Don't give feedback until *you have cooled down.* It's difficult to pick the right words when you're fuming. If you say the wrong words first, you only add fuel to the fire. Think through what you plan to say, and how you will say it. This planning will be more productive, and will prevent you or the employee from "flying off" at each other.

Don't overreact to the situation, especially if it is the first time there is a performance problem. I've seen managers act as if an employee committed a heinous crime when, in truth, the situation was rather minor.

People do make mistakes, and they sometimes know they made them. They may be nervous about it already. If it wasn't a mistake, then they did it on purpose. In this case it's not a situation for coaching, but one that leads to disciplining or firing. Create a learning situation for the employee, so the next time it will be done differently.

Address Behaviors Not Attitude

Let them know the purpose of the discussion. Tell them it is to discuss behaviors you have observed, and that you do care about them and their progress. Address observed service behaviors, and their causes or results. If you don't, you will fail to focus on the difference between the pre-set service standards and goals and the actual performance. Feedback, to be objective, has to be compared with an attainable standard. Otherwise, the person receiving it won't know where they are in relationship to the standard.

Describe the actual behavior you observed, or the results of that behavior or work process. This way the feedback is unbiased. You may not have actually witnessed a person giving the service, but you may know the result of it from a customer complaint or feedback card. Never discuss rumors.

Stay away from attitudes, character, or personality issues. Managers aren't psychiatrists, and they can't really understand the attitudes going on in an employee's mind. Don't try to guess what makes an employee tick.

Make it Visible

Whoever said a picture is worth a thousand words was right on target when it comes to giving feedback! Anytime you use graphs, charts, trackings, trends, or any visual display of performance, it serves as a powerful learning tool and motivator. Use different colors to show different trends, significant progress, or areas needing improvement.

Employees may argue with verbal feedback, but they seldom question the feedback that shows exactly how they are doing, related to the service goals set. Keep them appraised of where they were, where they are today, and where they need to be in the future. "In Workplace 2000, the results of work efforts will be tracked, measured, graphed, and exposed for all to see. There will be no doubt about who is contributing and who isn't" (Boyett & Conn, p. 82).

How to Give Feedback

An example of incorrect feedback is when a manager says to an employee, "Your attitude towards our customers is really poor." This is a vague statement. No specific service behavior is mentioned. Using this technique will only make employees feel they are under attack. They take it personally, and their reaction will instinctively be to defend themselves.

An example of a more effective method is: "I am really concerned about the behaviors I've observed, and the effects they may be having on our customers." "I have watched you . . ." (name specific behavior). "This is creating a situation where . . ." (describe the effects or consequences). "If you remember from our meeting or training . . ." (describe or demonstrate the correct method).

Asking a question afterwards can be very effective. Some questions that really work are:

- What may be causing this?
- What's getting in the way of this?
- What other way could you have reacted?
- What can I do to help in these areas?
- What can we do together to improve the situation?
- Is there anything else you need to do a better job?
- What can we do differently to achieve our goals?

In this example, the manager names a specific problem behavior he or she observed, and describes how this behavior affects the customers. The negative results on the customers (or employee, co-workers) need to be examined.

The manager referred back to the standards of behavior discussed at meetings or training. By using open-ended questions, you have given the employee a chance to respond, and also discuss how they will change. The questions show that the manager is offering to assist the employee in finding the cause and correcting the deficiency. There is a call for joint commitment and goal setting.

When you ask questions, it is critical to listen closely to the employees' opinions, or any other details related to the circumstances. In other words, don't interrupt. Let them get their whole side of the story out. They can give you information critical to the situation. There may be barriers or work processes preventing them from performing.

Don't Judge

Don't be judgmental. People have a tendency to judge and label behaviors they don't like. Try and eliminate words that are emotional and explosive. Using words such as "irresponsible" or "unreliable" can only create a more heated discussion. Again, stick with a physical description of what was observed.

Don't Magnify

Another thing people tend to do is exaggerate. If an employee is late on occasion, don't say "Why are you always late?" If they were always late, you would have fired them a long time ago!

Stay away from giving feedback in the form of a question. It reminds me of the old story about the supervisor who asked his frequently late employee, "Do you know what time we start work around here?" The employee answered innocently, "I don't know, I'm never here for that."

Instead, say: "On both Tuesday and Saturday, I observed that you were more than fifteen minutes late. Our house rules state that we are in at 7:30 a.m. and start work at 8:00. When you are late, other people have to cover for you, and our service suffers. Is there a home situation that is creating a difficulty for you, or can I do anything to help?"

Here, once again, specific observation of the behavior in question is discussed. The behavior then is compared to the pre-set standards. There is an offer to help. You want to show that you are there to support and provide solutions for your people.

Before the discussion is over, you must be sure the employee understands the correct service behavior or performance desired. Have them repeat the information back to you, or ask them how they will do it differently the next time. This is the only way you know that they know what to do. This doesn't always guaranty it will be done. It's best to document your conversations which can be included in your performance evaluation decisions.

Remember: it takes time to change old behaviors into new habits. The changes happen gradually, almost in stages. Further observations and follow-up discussions most likely will be necessary. Never take the changes in performance for granted.

How to Positively Reinforce Behavior

Many owners and managers look for the wrong behaviors. Unfortunately, people remember the negatives that they have heard far longer than the positives. Few managers spend time looking for the right behaviors. They simply don't know what to do when they see positive or exceptional behavior.

An important principle comes to us from the field of psychology: *Behavior followed by a positive consequence will result in more of that behavior.* If employees are doing things right, and you recognize them for it, in most cases, you will get more of that behavior. But, the opposite of this is also true. If behavior is followed by no consequence or a negative consequence, the behavior will decrease. If managers do not recognize people for doing a good job, the behavior tends to decrease. Or, if they have an employee who is a superstar, they reward them by piling on more work. This is the quickest way to destroy motivation.

Bear Bryant, the great, late football coach of the University of Alabama was clear cut as to what it took to motivate people. The Bear, in his unique basso profundo voice, declared, "In order to motivate, all you have to do is give people credit where credit is due. If anything bad happens, I did it. If anything semi-good happens, we did it. If anything great happens, we all did it. That's all it takes."

In my front line training seminars on customer service I ask the question, "How many of you want to be excellent at what you do?" This is always followed by everyone in the group raising their hands and nodding with enthusiasm. I then follow with, "How many of you want to be just average?" This is always followed by silence, with no hands. However, in a seminar with a Fortune 500 company, a young woman raised her hand after the second question. I asked her why she wanted to be just average. I never will forget her answer. She said, very strongly , "If I am really excellent at everything thing I do, they just keep giving me more to do. I wouldn't mind doing it, but they never reward me or thank me for it. They just keep piling it on."

What a powerful message! It is *imperative* that you spend time verbally recognizing, praising, and reinforcing the behaviors you want. If you are not used to looking for the good things taking place at your company, then make a commitment to do just that, everyday. Take fifteen minutes a day to walk around and find something good to reinforce and let people know they are doing a good job. As Mary Kay Ash, founder of Mary Kay Cosmetics said, "There are two things people want more than sex and money: recognition and praise" (Nelson, p. 9).

If you are not used to praising, complimenting, and thanking you may find it hard at first. If you have a history of talking down to your people (and you know who you are), this will be really tough for you. Your employees may be shocked at first, and they may be a little skeptical. However, there is an easy way to fix that. In a meeting, admit to your staff that you have said some wrong things in the past, and you would like to change the way you communicate. This has the effect of "wiping the slate" so that you can start over again. Obviously, you have to be sincere because employees will be watching. With a little practice, it will become second nature.

Don't Wait for Perfection

Don't wait for the desired changes to be perfect or error free. Praise and recognize every sign or step of improvement. Also, recognize efforts towards improvement, even if the improvement is slight. Otherwise, some employees may give up. Tell people, "I really like the way you've been working towards improving your . . . (name the service behaviors). I see it and I appreciate your efforts. Keep up the progress, and pretty soon you'll have mastered it."

Be Specific

Describe a specific behavior that you observed. Don't be vague or general. Don't say "I really appreciate the way you handled that situation." Instead, say, "It was really great how you handled that irate customer. You stayed calm, listened to them, and solved their problem. You turned the situation around, and they went away satisfied."

Be Genuine

When you have described and reinforced the specific behavior, don't add any negatives. Let the good act stand alone. It has more meaning. Managers often will say something positive, and then they will add on a negative. Or, they will the use the situation to assign the employee some new assignment or extra work. This only destroys your credibility the next time you attempt to reinforce behavior. Using mere flattery won't get you anywhere. The comments must be genuine.

Use Positive Gossip

Suppose another employee or a customer tells you about a situation where someone was exceptional, but you didn't see it. What should you do? Let the employee know who told you about it, and what they said. This let's them know that not only was it seen and noted, but someone else thought it was so good they had to tell you. When employees know that people are saying positive things about them, its impact skyrockets their self esteem and motivates them to new heights.

Let Them Brag

When someone has done something unique, difficult, or outstanding, mention it at a meeting so they are recognized in front of their peers. You may also want to give them a few minutes to talk about themselves, and how they accomplished their feat. Most people love to talk about their accomplishments.

However, ask them before the meeting if they want to talk about it so they aren't embarrassed. With so many ethnic groups in the workforce, some, particularly Asian Americans and Native Americans, don't like to brag about accomplishments because it just embarrasses them.

Phone It In

One of the necessary evils of being a manager and/or owner are the travel requirements. You can use this opportunity to give positive reinforcement or praise. One clever C.E.O. I know makes it a habit, when calling in for his messages and discussing the day's events, to be put through to someone who has done something exceptional. He tells them what city he is in, and he tells the employee he just wanted to thank them for a job well done. Sometimes he will leave a message on their voice mail. He varies the timing and frequency so employees never know when they might get a call. It has a dramatic, powerful, and positive effect. A variation on this motivator is to fax a long distance note to praise people. It may be a little more impersonal, but it still has a positive impact.

Remove Tasks They Dislike

We always think of giving something as a method of positive reinforcement. An often overlooked method of increasing positive behavior is to take away something that the employee does not enjoy doing. There may be a task that is so boring, aggravating, or frustrating that the employee finds it absolutely distasteful. Ask them first if there is a different way of doing the task that would make it more enjoyable. If not, try delegating the task to someone else. If it is a task no one likes to do, share or rotate the task on a continuous basis.

Giving high quality feedback and positive reinforcement means being able to say the right thing at the right time. This takes a little practice. But it's like constantly using a muscle; eventually the muscle becomes stronger. It is that strength that creates loyal, committed, and productive people who will serve your customers the way you want them to be served.

Quick Chapter Tips

1. Use feedback as a valuable tool for improving employee performance which, in turn, will improve quality of service.

2. Be sensitive to foreign born employees. Each culture is different. Learn about their values and attitudes before giving them feedback or motivating them.

3. Feedback works best when it is done as a learning experience. If done properly it will motivate employees to make positive changes.

4. Write out the standards and goals your organization expects and make sure every employee has that information. Measure results and give feedback comparing the results to your standards.

5. The sooner people receive feedback, the easier it is for them to make changes.

6. When giving corrective feedback, do it in private. Don't humiliate or embarrass an employee. Make sure your anger has cooled before approaching the person.

7. Give feedback about their *behavior* not their attitude. Compare their behavior to your organization's pre-set service standards.

8. Use graphs, charts, or any other means to visually display employees' performance. Show them where they were and where they need to be.

9. When giving feedback, don't be judgmental or magnify the situation. Use specific observations of their behavior.

10. Be sure to praise and encourage employees' efforts and attempts to change at each sign of improvement.

10

Rewards and Recognition: The Twin Factors That Drive Outstanding Service

What are the real reasons people work? A mistaken assumption is that people work for a paycheck. In reality, employees don't work for a paycheck, but to *prevent the lack of a paycheck.*

In times of downsizing, organizational flattening, and cost cutting, benefits and job security rank right at the top in importance. In the November 1992 issue of Inc. magazine, a multi-study analysis proves this to be correct. However, these studies show that interesting and meaningful work are also at or near the top in significance; while high income ranks toward the middle or bottom of the categories (Caggiano, 1992).

One recent report by the National Science Foundation examined over 300 studies about job satisfaction, performance, and pay. The studies overwhelmingly concluded that motivation and productivity increase when performance and pay are linked. The employees' sense of achievement and gratification were also greater. In one case, performance feedback alone raised productivity 43%. When rewards and incentives were combined with positive reinforcement and feedback, productivity rose an incredible 64%!

Today's workforce looks for a sense of meaningful achievement in their work; a sense of purpose. This fulfills their intrinsic needs. Employees look also for external motivation for performing a job well. They need something that confirms their accomplishments. Rewards and recognition from management and peers supply the motivation they crave. *These twin motivators send a message that service excellence is valued, and employees are valued as major contributors to it.*

In the real world, not many employees receive rewards or recognition for a job well done. Is it any wonder that few workers see the connection between rewards and their performance? So many workers feel this connection is paramount to job satisfaction and daily meaning in their work lives, and yet, they aren't getting it!

As the workforce ages, and less qualified workers come in, your biggest concern will be preventing turnover and keeping quality people. You don't have many options available to modify people's behavior or satisfy their needs. The old autocratic way of bossing people around just won't work. You have to find ways that are effective to stop the revolving door.

The message is clear. *Reward and recognize your people for exceptional behavior if you want them to repeat those behaviors.* No longer will today's workers accept being overlooked all year, until it becomes time for a performance evaluation. They want immediate feedback, and often. This may be the most critical element in creating satisfied and service-committed workers within the new workforce.

Today's young and changing workforce is familiar with a reward system because it was often used by their parents to get them to do family chores. Teachers used it all the time to modify behavior. It has become the most solidly-based and proven management concept. It delivers an incredibly positive impact.

Some Basic Considerations

Review Your Present System

To determine whether your people are getting the rewards they need take inventory of your current reward and recognition systems. This will give you a baseline or starting point. You need this information if you are to carry out a reward and recognition system that will work.

Begin by asking yourself the following questions:

1. Have you carefully defined what service behaviors and skills are necessary to achieve service excellence?

2. Have you done a recent survey of what behaviors and skills are being routinely rewarded and recognized (if any) within your organization?

3. Do these two lists remotely resemble each other?

A common mistake is that rewards and recognition are not tied into the actual wanted service behaviors and skills. One electronics retailer brought me in to consult with them on what they thought was a training problem. Their employees were increasing their sales each month, but at the same time, the firm was losing money. The number of customer complaints was rising at an alarming rate. They were getting a reputation for bad service in spite of increased sales.

When we examined their rewards system we found a discrepancy between what was being rewarded and what was expected. The employees were being rewarded with incentives to raise sales through monthly goal setting. Each month the goal was raised a little higher. They received an incentive for achieving their goal, and for sales above the set goal.

The employees thought only about one thing: raising their sales and getting the reward. It didn't matter what they sold or what the customer needed. The only thing that mattered was the sales volume. As a result, the company's customer service began to suffer.

In this case, one behavior was overly rewarded, and the other was ignored. The rewarded behavior became the permanent behavior, at the expense of good service. The desired behavior of good customer service was overlooked, so it was never achieved.

Training alone could not solve this problem. The entire reward system had to be changed so that quantity and quality were in balance. Sales needed to go up, but service couldn't suffer in the process. We then designed a reward system where sales coupled with service were rewarded; but sales lacking service were not. This, along with proper service training, set the firm back on track.

In other words, rewards and recognition are often based on nothing related to service performance. People are rewarded for longevity, cost-of-living adjustments (COLA'S), automatic Christmas bonuses, or many other factors that have no relationship to customer satisfaction.

These incentives alone are not bad. *However, there is nothing less motivating than when you lump together your average or non-performing people with your top performers, and treat them as equals!* Realize that when the rewards are continually expected and received, they are less appreciated.

Define and Train the Service Behaviors

What service behaviors and skills do you want from your employees? We asked this same question in the chapter on training. If you determine that your service behaviors and skills have not been defined, so that all employees are working from the same standards, then you must start here. Let them know what the expected behavior is, what it looks like, and what the expected results are. If employees don't understand what it looks like, or how to perform it, they won't do it. Defining standards of behavior and then training employees to meet them is crucial.

Be Realistic

The service behavior being rewarded must be within control of the people performing the behavior. In other words, the employees must be able to learn the new behavior. There is no point in setting standards of behavior that are impossible to reach. The behaviors must be understood and attainable. Remember to be realistic in your expectations.

Find Out What Is Meaningful

The next step is to brainstorm for a variety of monetary and non-monetary rewards to motivate your staff. What rewards are meaningful and important to your employees? What are the best ways to recognize them for their efforts? The most effective way to find out is to ask them individually, or have them fill out a questionnaire. Remember, what you may think is a reward often is not to an employee. So, determine what rewards your people value.

Make It Easy to Create and Administer

Although there are many complicated, well thought out programs that work very well in large and small corporations, we still find that some of the best programs are the simple ones. Start with the basics of spontaneous rewards that take little planning. These programs also require little, if any, record keeping.

One small business owner we know gives out comments on little yellow sticky notes. When an employee gets five, the owner gives them a cash reward. When they get ten, they have their choice of certain gifts from a merchandise catalog. The gift choices change after fifteen or twenty notes. It's simple, easy to keep record of, and a real incentive to people. It has helped him cut turnover from 120% to 47%!

Don't create a paper monster that overwhelms you! As time goes on, you can develop and grow your program in many different ways, limited only by your creativity and time. The amount of time you spend will result in cutting turnover, as well as building repeat business from satisfied customers.

Get Employees Involved in Designing it

Just as you asked employees what rewards are meaningful to them, ask their advice on the best way to create and implement a program. They will give you some good insights into what is fair, as well as fun, exciting, and motivating. They will be quick to let you know what will lower morale or create conflicts. Their input, feedback, and support are critical to success. And, consulting employees drives home the message, *"Your opinion counts."*

Ask questions such as:

- "What do you like about it?"
- "What would you change?"
- "How would you strengthen it?"
- "What does it lack?"
- "How can we be sure it will work?"

Guidelines for Rewarding and Recognizing

Set Clear Goals and Objectives

Let employees know exactly what the purpose of the program is, and what you are trying to achieve. Let them know the quality and service goals, cost savings, or productivity outcomes that you want. In addition to customer satisfaction and quality, set goals for sales, attendance, on-time performance, and safety. Explain that the rewards and recognition will be tied to specific goals in these areas, as well as unique and innovative suggestions made by them.

If you find that everyone is being rewarded for all the goals you have set, then perhaps you have set the standards too low. You need to re-evaluate your system, and re-set your goals and objectives to a higher level.

Once You Start

In order to be effective, your rewards and recognition program must become a continuous process, not just an occasional event. If employees find you aren't serious about the awards program, they'll soon forget about any future program you implement. It will become business as usual. You will lose the main reason for having such a system, which is to improve service and performance.

Communicate the Purpose

Communicate everything about the program that will help make it work. Capture their attention, and get them *excited* about its objectives. Inform them of the kinds of rewards and recognition that will be available. Let them know that the program is not designed to punish anyone. Don't confuse them by giving mixed messages. Their early reactions and perceptions are critical to its success.

Use Monetary and Non-Monetary Rewards

Although cash awards are effective, desirable, and easy to administer, they don't have quite the same meaning as non-monetary rewards. Cash does not have memory value; and sometimes comes to be expected. It may go into the bank, but often it's spent. Employees quickly forget the reward.

For non-monetary rewards, it's more effective to have something that grabs their attention, and keeps it. If the award is enjoyed with their family, the employee never forgets the hard work they did to get it, along with the feeling of achievement.

The best kind of merchandise rewards have a positive, lasting value, and are practical as well as useful. These express your appreciation for their efforts. Travel awards, merchandise, and awards that create status and recognition stay in their memory. People can talk about them with their friends and relatives.

For example, if you offer employees a $500 cash award, they won't turn it down. But if you offer them a weekend for two at a nearby fine resort with all expenses paid, the perceived value is much higher. In addition, the cash costs more, as people have to pay taxes on the cash amount. Given a choice, employees feel the trip or award are more exciting than the cash.

Use food as a reward. The possibilities are endless! It is useful, enjoyable, and can be shared with their families. Gifts can include certificates to restaurants, or food delivered to their home.

In my experience, the most effective reward and recognition programs have a blend of both money and gift awards. Mixing cash, gift certificates, merchandise, travel, recognition plaques and trophies, fun events, and celebrations keeps the program alive and inspiring. Again, having your employees involved in the planning will tell you what they want, and what is rewarding for them.

Do It Now

Reward or recognize the desired behavior as soon as possible after the behavior is exhibited. The longer you wait to praise an employee, the less dramatic its impact. Rewarding someone weeks later doesn't reinforce the exceptional behavior. Their motivation to repeat the behavior declines.

Just Say Thanks

In surveys, employees tell us they aren't given enough appreciation for a job well done. Start by just giving a simple thank-you. Write it on a little yellow sticky or on a pay check envelope. If you have artistic talent create a colorful thank-you card for them. It costs absolutely nothing. Or, send a letter of thanks, appreciation and support to the employee's family when they have given extra time on a project done well.

Show how much you appreciate their efforts. Do some part of their job for a week, especially something they don't like. Get creative! Buy their lunch for a week, or wash their car for them in the company lot. Make a big and fun deal out of it. Saying thanks in different ways goes very far in reinforcing behaviors.

Match the Results

All achievements and their results should be treated equally. So, the rewards or recognitions must match the goal and those results. If an employee performed a small, but extra task, they deserve a reward, but something on the small side. For example, If they stayed late one night to help you finish a report, that deserves one type of reward. However, if they took on a three month project, and had outstanding results, that deserves another type of reward. Always look at the significance of the results, and the time and effort the employee put into it.

Reward Often and in Small Amounts

Rewards, of any kind, should come frequently and in small amounts. If you only recognize the behavior occasionally, you are less apt to have employees behave the way you want them to behave. If you reward often in large amounts, it soon becomes too costly to your company. Small, but frequent recognition fosters fun, and creates greater motivation.

At the same time, you don't want to reward so often that it becomes meaningless. Remember, we are talking about rewarding for exceptional behavior and performance that goes above your set standards.

Vary Timing and Type

Vary the rewards in both frequency and type. If you continually recognize the behaviors with the same rewards or praise, they begin to lose their effectiveness. An assortment of rewards and recognition at different and unexpected times keeps the behavior consistent, and generates enthusiasm. Use the element of surprise whenever possible. It creates fun, goodwill, and lessens stress.

Be Fair and Equitable

Does everyone have the same opportunity to get the same rewards or recognition? This includes unseen employees such as bookkeepers, janitors, clerks, and stock people. As the number of part-timers and temporary employees grows, don't forget their valuable contributions. Rewards must be available, fair, and equitable to everyone.

In rewarding superior performance, don't forget the everyday, consistently good performer. These people are like steady anchors that can always be depended upon.

Does every employee get a reward equal in value for achieving the same results? Giving two employees rewards of unequal value for the same performance makes employees feel they are being treated unfairly. This destroys employee morale and loyalty.

Never reward the non-performers. If you don't link excellent performance to the reward, you are simply rewarding mediocrity. If you reward average behavior, that's what you get more of! Always remember: the most rewards go to the best performers.

Reward Individuals and Teams

One of the drawbacks of reward programs is that they are designed unintentionally to pit employees against each other, as they compete for the awards. One of the ways to stop this conflict is to recognize team efforts.

When you reward at both the individual level and team levels, it sends out two messages. First, you value team pride. Second, your people must learn to work together as interacting teams, and serve each other as internal customers. They all need to pull together. When people pull together as a team and achieve a synergy that is impossible alone, they need to be recognized for their achievements. Just as you can have employee of the month, quarter, or year, you can have department, team, or unit of the month, quarter, or year.

Time Off as a Reward

Entrepreneur Magazine (December, 1991) discusses a survey done by Hilton Hotels of over one thousand workers. The results showed that 48% of them would consent to an extra day off each week, although they would not receive pay for it. Today's workforce values its free time, and would have more of it in return for less money. The message is that you can use time off as a very desirable reward.

There are many different ways to use time off as a reward. One of the most effective ways is to use it spontaneously, just after someone has done something exceptional. Giving them the rest of the day off, a longer or extra break, a two hour lunch, a three day weekend, or an extra vacation day has an incredible impact on reinforcing service behaviors.

Consider using flex time as a reward. With today's rapidly changing family structure, people have different life styles and varying needs. Many would love the opportunity to have more flexible work hours to care for their family, or attend classes, or simply relax.

Celebrate Achievement

The final link in making your rewards and recognition system work, and in forming new behaviors, is to spotlight those exhibiting exceptional behavior, or those who have shown the greatest improvement. Celebrate their achievements. Recognize that their contributions have made a valuable difference. Celebrations let people know they are vital to the company, and they are an integral part of things you value in your business.

Announce special awards and large rewards at special events, parties, or picnics. At banquets, give special service recognition, certificates, plaques, trophies, merchandise, tickets to sporting events, or for travel.

A side benefit of "spotlighting" is that it makes poor performance even more glaring. Employees not up to standard are often motivated to improve service performance. It automatically builds peer pressure. Those not interested in improving, for whatever reason, often quit, rather than become humiliated or outcasts to co-workers.

With today's employees having many diverse ethnic backgrounds, you need to be careful. Some cultures do not respond well to public recognition. They view it as an embarrassment. This is particularly true of some people from Asian and Native American backgrounds. With these employees, as well as any others you may not be sure about, be sensitive to individual needs. Always ask how they want to be rewarded before embarking on any public recognition or a reward ceremony.

Showcase Superior Behavior

Naming employee or manager of the month, or quarter, or department of the month or quarter, is not a new concept, but it still works extremely well. Tie it to a criteria of quality goals or service behaviors.

Reward them with the first parking space near the door, or under a special canopy with a large sign stating Employee Of The Month or quarter, and their name. The canopy is a welcome relief in Florida and other states where it's hot, or rains frequently.

Make exceptional employees highly visible by putting their photos on bulletin boards, in display cases, or company newsletters. Display letters to the employees from satisfied customers or, display a recognition letter from the company president.

Many small businesses we have worked with have set up a bulletin board near the door, known as the "Wall of Fame." This wall is for posting and recognizing anything positive about their people and their customer service efforts. They want their customers to see that they value their customers and their employees. List achievements of your staff's family in the organization's newsletter and post them on the wall. This can include such accomplishments as their children making the school honor roll or a spouse's promotion.

This board may include any special customer letters that were sent in as a result of exceptional service. It may include their customer service index which shows the weekly percentage of customer satisfaction. You can also post any special letters coming from top management about your staff's service or performance.

Include special events or recognition that happen in your people's lives. You let both your staff and your customers know that you value your employees' achievements apart from the workplace. Birthdays, anniversaries, marriages, newborns, completion of school or special certification, public service recognition, or anything important can be placed here. Add these to your company newsletter also. Remember, how you treat your people is directly reflected in how they treat your customers.

Make slides of superior employees or innovative teams. Flash those slides on the cafeteria wall for a certain time period. I've been in companies that do this in the lobby or reception area. Customers are curious and inevitably ask questions. They have a warm response to the answers about your employee recognition. Your customers like to do business with companies who take care of their employees.

Other companies we consulted with create an employee photo book with all employees having an 8 X 10 glossy photo in a loose leaf binder. It is placed on a table in the lobby area. You can also write about special individuals or teams in your company newsletter. This can be placed in a special column entitled "Service Above and Beyond."

Consider giving superior employees a highly visible work area for a month. Spotlight them by giving them noticeable responsibilities such as helping out with orientation or training. Reward them with a special assignment that is both challenging and satisfying.

Monitor and Measure

Monitor your program to see if it is effective. Is it improving the quality of your service and performance? Did the program achieve what you wanted by a certain date? If not, discuss the program with employees. Find out what they liked or did not like. Determine what you can do to strengthen the program. By all means, do not abandon it. Improve it to be more realistic, fair, and meaningful to all employees.

Creating a successful reward and recognition system requires time and money. Truly, it is an investment. The dividends it brings are: greater employee self-esteem, increased job satisfaction, higher innovation and creativity, improved morale, and greater employee loyalty.

The total return on your investment is: higher customer satisfaction, increased productivity, and improved performance. Any investment that gives such a high return is well worth the cost.

Quick Chapter Tips

1. Rewarding and recognizing for exceptional behavior is critical for motivating employees.

2. Determine which behaviors and skills are currently being rewarded. Do they match what customers need and want?

3. Reward for both quantity and quality of service. Tie rewards to service performance.

4. Use monetary and non-monetary rewards that are meaningful to employees.

5. Create a rewards and recognition system that is easy to implement with simple recordkeeping. Once you start a program it must be continuous and ongoing.

6. When designing the program, get your employees' input and opinions. It will make them feel valued.

7. Communicate the objectives, intent, and scope of the program to all employees.

8. Don't wait to reward or recognize excellence. Do it as soon as possible.

9. Reward in small doses and often. Vary the kinds of rewards. Surprise employees—it's fun and exciting!

10. Be sure that the reward matches the achievement. Be fair and equitable to everyone. Don't leave anyone out.

11. Reward team behaviors as well as individual behaviors.

12. Have celebrations to shine the spotlight on exceptional employees but be sensitive to various ethnic groups that may dread public recognition.

13. Create a "wall of fame" to recognize workers achievements, excellence, and special events in people's lives.

14. Keep monitoring and measuring your program for its effectiveness and make any changes that may be needed.

Specific Rewards and Recognition

Popular Merchandise

- Cash (with taxes prepaid) or gift certificates
- Mystery shoppers award instant cash for exceptional service
- Pay for important service (e.g. child tutoring, house-cleaning, babysitting)
- Theater or concert tickets
- Sporting events
- Music, art, or cultural events tickets
- Dinner for two
- T-shirts, jackets, caps with company logo
- Plaques, trophies, lapel pins
- Watches, clocks (engraved), jewelry
- Glassware, ceramics, mugs
- Electronic devices
- Desk and office accessories
- Sporting goods, luggage
- Travel
- Gift, card, or cake for birthday, anniversary or child birth
- Fruit or gift basket
- Seminar or conference attendance
- Flowers or balloons
- Books, magazines, video or audio-tapes
- Raffle or lottery tickets

Popular Recognition

- Employee or manager of the month, quarter, or year
- Department, team, or unit of the month, quarter, or year
- Service maniac of the month, quarter or year
- Service rookie of the month, quarter, or year
- Service martyr of the week award
- ABCD Award for Above and Beyond the Call of Duty
- GEM Award for Going the Extra Mile
- MVP or Most Valuable Player award for team or unit member
- Customer Service All Star Team of the Year Award
- Lifesaver of the Year Award
- Service idea of the month, quarter, or year
- Recognition awards at luncheons or dinners
- Social events such as picnics, barbecues (where management cooks), or parties that give recognition
- Employee photos on bulletin boards, newsletters, or photo book
- Special letters of recognition on bulletin boards or newsletters
- Appreciation letters or telegrams mailed home
- Peer recognition awards for special efforts, teamwork, or internal service
- "No Reason At All Party" just to say "thanks"
- Rent a billboard to honor an employee, team or your entire company
- Cost savings idea of the month, quarter, or year
- Give employees more work they enjoy
- Put employee on special project or task force they want
- Time off for exceptional behavior or achievement

References

Astin, Alexander W. and Staff. "The American Freshman: National Norms for Fall." Los Angeles, CA.: Higher Education Research Institute, U.C.L.A.,1991, 1992, 1993, 1994 (flyer).

Barciela, Grace. "Investing in Employees Bolsters the Bottom Line." *Miami Herald*, June 11, 1995, pp. 1K & 6K.

Barciela, Grace. "Barnett Tops List of Woman-Friendly Firms." *Miami Herald,* June 14, 1995, pp. 1c & 3c.

Bass, Bernard M. and Avolio, Bruce J. "Shattering the Glass Ceiling: Women Make Better Managers." *Human Resource Management,* Winter, 1994, pp. 557-558.

Bennis, Warren, and Nanus, Burt. *Leaders: The Strategies for Taking Charge.* New York, NY.: Harper & Row, 1985.

Bishop, J. "Achievement, Test Scores, and Relative Wages." Conference Paper, Washington, DC.: American Enterprise Institute for Public Policy Research, 1989.

Block, Peter. *The Empowered Manager: Positive Skills at Work.* San Francisco, CA.: Jossey Bass, 1987.

Boyett, Joseph H., and Conn, Henry P. *Workplace 2000: The Revolution Reshaping American Business.* New York, NY.: Plume, 1991.

Caggiano, Christopher. "What Do Workers Want." *Inc.,* November, 1992, p. 101.

Carnevale, Anthony P. "America and the New Economy." Washington, DC.: Government Printing Office, 1990 p. 4.

Copeland, Lennie. "Four by Four." *Training & Development Journal,* February, 1989, pp. 17-18.

"Corporate Women." *Business Week,* June 8, 1992, pp. 78-83.

Deming, W. Edwards. *Out of the Crisis.* Boston, MA.: Center for Advanced Engineering Study, M.I.T., 1986.

Desatnick, Robert. *Managing to Keep the Customer.* San Francisco, CA.: Jossey Bass, 1987.

Desatnick, Robert. Adopted from "Most Important Job-Related Behaviors for Success in a Customer-Oriented Organization." Personal Communication, July, 1988.

Dey, Eric L.; Astin, Alexander W.; and Korn, William S. *The American Freshman: Twenty Five Year Trends.* Los Angeles, CA.: Higher Education Research Institute, U.C.L.A., 1991.

Dixon, Pam. "Jobs on the Web." *Sky Magazine,* May 1995, pp. 130-138.

Doyle, Kevin. "Young and Restless." *Incentive,* June, 1993, pp. 76-77, & 83.

Dunn, William. *The Baby Bust: A Generation Comes of Age.* Ithaca, NY.: American Demographic Books, 1993.

Francis, Dave, and Young, Don. *Improving Work Groups: A Practical Manual for Team Building.* San Diego CA.: Pfeiffer and Company, 1992.

Fyock, Catherine D. *Get the Best: How to Recruit the People You Want.* Homewood, IL.: Business One Irwin, 1993.

Garfield, Charles. *Peak Performers.* New York, NY.: Morrow, 1986.

Garvin, Glenn. "No Fruit, No Shirts, No Service: The Real World Consequences of Closed Borders." *Miami Herald,* April 2, 1995, pp. 1C & 5C.

Jamieson, David and O'Mara, Julie. *Managing Workforce 2000: Gaining the Diversity Advantage.* San Francisco, CA.: Jossey-Bass, 1991.

Johnston, William, B. and Packer, Arnold, H. *Workforce 2000: Work and Workers for the 21st Century.* Indianapolis, IN.: Hudson Institute, 1987.

Loden, Marilyn, and Rosener, Judy B. *Workforce America: Managing Employee Diversity as a Vital Resource.* Homewood, IL.: Business One Irwin, 1991.

Losyk, Bob, and Preziosi, Bob. "The Customer Service Audit." Ft. Lauderdale, Fl.: Innovative Training Solutions, Inc., 1990.

Miller, William H. "Employers Wrestle With Dumb Kids." *Industry Week,* July 4, 1988, pp. 47-52.

Murphy, Terence. "Boomers, Busters, and 50-Plussers: Managing the New Generation Gaps." *Working Woman,* July, 1991, p. 44.

National Center on Education and the Economy. *America's Choice: High Skills or Low Wages!* Rochester, NY.: National Center on Education and the Economy, 1990.

Nelson, Bob. *1001 Ways to Reward Your Employees.* New York, NY.: Workman Publishing, 1994.

New York Times Service. "Employers Wary of Youth in Workplace, Survey Says." *Miami Herald,* February 20, 1995, p. 10A.

Peterson, Karen S. "In Balancing Act, Scale Tips Toward Family." *USA Today,* Jan 24, 1995, p. 2A.

Pilenzo, Ronald C. "Preparing for the Workforce of Tomorrow." *Modern Office Technology,* August, 1990, p. 49.

Reuters Time Service. "Investing in Workers Pays Off Big, Study Shows." *Miami Herald,* June 7, 1995, pp. 1C & 5C.

Samon, Katherine Ann. "The Brash Pack: How to Manage the Twenty Something Generation." *Working Woman,* August, 1990, pp. 68-69.

Solomon, Charlene Marmer. "Managing the Baby Busters." *Personnel Journal,* March, 1992, pp. 56-58.

"The Age Wave: An Interview with Ken Dychtwald." *Training & Development Journal,* February, 1990, pp. 23-29.

Therrien, Lois; Carson, Teresa; Hamilton, Joan; and Hurlock, Jim. "What Do Woman Want? A Company They Can Call Their Own." *Business Week,* December, 1989, p. 60.

Thiederman, Sondra. *Bridging Cultural Barriers for Corporate Success.* New York, NY.: Lexington Books, 1991.

U.S. Bureau of the Census. *Demographic Changes in the United States: 1990.* Washington, DC.: U.S. Government Printing Office, 1990.

Varney, Glenn, H. *Building Productive Teams.* San Francisco, CA.: Jossey Bass, 1989.

Zaldivar, R.A. "Up Escalator is Becoming a Slow Ride." *Miami Herald,* January 30, 1995, pp. 1A & 9A.

Index

Give the Gift of
Increased Business Success to Your
Friends and Colleagues

CHECK YOUR LEADING BOOKSTORE OR ORDER HERE

YES, I want ____ copies of *Managing A Changing Workforce: Achieving Outstanding Service with Today's Employees* at $24.95 each, plus $3 shipping per book (Florida residents please add $1.50 state sales tax per book). Canadian orders must be accompanied by a postal money order in U.S. funds. Allow 15 days for delivery.

☐ **YES**, I am interested in having Bob Losyk speak or give a seminar to my company, association, school, or organization. Please send information.

☐ **YES**, I am interested in Bob's Employee Opinion Surveys, Customer Service Audits, Interview Questions, audio tapes and video tapes. Please send information.

My check or money order for $____ is enclosed.
Please charge my ☐ Visa ☐ MasterCard ☐ AmEx

Name _____

Organization _____

Phone _____

Address _____

City/State/Zip _____

Card # _____

Exp. Date _____ Signature _____

Please make your check payable and return to:
Workplace Trends Publishing Company
10396 S.W. 17th Drive, Davie, FL 33324
Fax: (305) (954 after August '96) 424-0625

Or call with your credit card order:
(305) (954 after August '96) 236-6863